OUR
FUTURE
KING

OUR FUTURE KING

Peter Lane

Arthur Barker Limited London
A subsidiary of Weidenfeld (Publishers) Limited

For Patrick, Dominic, Richard, Elizabeth and Kate
in memory of their father and my brother –
a true prince from Wales who has a greater crown
(2 Tim. 4:6–7)

Published in Great Britain by
Arthur Barker Limited
11 St John's Hill, London SW11

ISBN 0 213 16679 8

Printed in Great Britain by
Morrison & Gibb Ltd
London and Edinburgh

Contents

Illustrations

I

The Early Years
1948-52

Prince Charles was born on the night of Sunday 14 November 1948, less than a year after the marriage of his mother, Princess Elizabeth, to the young naval officer Philip Mountbatten. In the early summer the announcement that the heir-apparent was expecting a child had given late October as the expected date of birth. However, the unborn royal was a long time coming. Public interest in the Princess' expected baby was heightened by the fact that it would be the first baby born at Buckingham Palace for sixty-two years. The radio news and reports in the newspapers had told the public that Sir William Gilliat, the Princess' gynaecologist, had been called to the Palace on Saturday and had stayed overnight. It seemed that the birth was imminent. During the whole of that grey, chilly Sunday people had been gathering outside the Palace. Some of them saw the King's physician arrive at the Palace in the morning; any excitement caused by this news was dampened by the subsequent announcement that he had left after only a short visit to the Princess.

By 7 pm there were between three and four thousand people outside the Palace. Some stood on the steps of the Victoria Memorial, others climbed on to the statue itself – even though there was nothing to be seen. Inside the Palace the young Princess had been taken by her husband and the midwife, Sister Helen Rowe, to the Buhl Room, which had once been part of the children's living quarters but had been made into a surgical ward for an operation on King George VI. Prince Philip, anxious as only the expectant father of a first child can be, but feeling that he could be of no further use, left the Princess with the doctors and midwife. He changed into flannels and went to play squash in the Palace courts with his private secretary, Michael Parker.

After a swim in the adjoining pool, Prince Philip was still on the squash court when, at 9.15 pm, an aide ran to tell him that the baby had been born. He rushed to the sitting-room where King George and Queen Elizabeth were waiting. The very

I

popular royal couple had taken great pleasure in the wedding of their elder daughter in 1947 and it is easy to imagine the happiness with which they greeted the news of the birth of their first grandson and eventual heir to the throne. Queen Elizabeth was heard to say: 'Isn't it wonderful,' – a remark which many a grandmother has been known to make. The delighted father then went to see his wife and baby. From some hiding place he picked up a bouquet of roses and carnations to give Princess Elizabeth as soon as she recovered from the anaesthetic. Later that evening he poured champagne for the Palace staff and the royal family's personal staff – as might be expected from a proud father and relieved husband.

Outside the Palace the police kept the crowds back to allow the guards to march up and down on their beat, at that time still outside the Palace gates. But the ones in front were pushed forward by latecomers who had heard on the evening news that the birth was expected that day. Finally a door in the Palace opened, a page wearing royal blue livery crossed the courtyard and spoke to a police inspector, who shouted to the crowd: 'It's a prince!' The announcement was greeted with a roar of welcome. At 11 pm a notice was put up on a board: 'The Princess Elizabeth, Duchess of Edinburgh, was safely delivered of a Prince at 9.14 pm today. Her Royal Highness and her son are both doing well.'

News of the child's arrival had been telephoned through to his great-grandmother, Queen Mary, at Marlborough House. She had been ill with influenza and had not seen her grand-daughter for some weeks. The eighty-one-year-old Queen insisted on being driven to the Palace where she had lived with her husband, George v, for the twenty-six splendid years of his reign. Now, at almost midnight, she insisted on going to see the new Prince, the heir in whose tiny hands lay the future of the dynasty of which she had been such a proud member. When she left, the crowds outside the gates cheered and shouted their congratulations to the royal great-grandmother. She noted in her diary: 'I gave the baby a silver gilt cup and cover which George III had given to a godson in 1780, so that I gave a present from my great-grandfather to my great-grandson 168 years later.'

By this time the floodlights in Trafalgar Square had been changed to blue in honour of the baby Prince, the crowds outside the Palace and down the Mall were singing, demanding: 'We want Philip,' and dozens of taxis and cars were tooting their horns in good-humoured mood. After Queen Mary had left the Palace a police car moved slowly among the crowd, the loudspeaker repeating the message: 'Ladies and gentlemen, it is requested from the Palace that we have a little quietness, if you please.' But little notice was taken for a couple of hours more until finally a senior royal official came out to say, 'Please, Princess Elizabeth wants some rest. Prince Philip is with her and there will be nothing more tonight.' Slowly, unwillingly but cheerfully, the crowds began to make their way home – most of them on foot since the last buses and tube trains had gone.

The staff at the Palace sent news of the Prince's birth to friends, relations, governors and ambassadors; the first message was sent, according to the ancient privileges of the City, to the Lord Mayor of London. Public announcement of the birth was made through notices signed by the Home Secretary, James Chuter Ede, and pinned outside the Home Office in Whitehall and on the door of the Mansion House in the City. For many centuries it had been the custom for a privy councillor to be present at the actual birth of a royal baby with any claim to the throne. This embarrassing practice had taken firm shape after James II's Catholic wife, Mary of Modena, was alleged to have produced a changeling son as heir to the throne in 1688. Ever since that event – which supposedly took place in full view of many privy councillors gathered around the royal bed – the home secretary had been summoned to witness personally the birth of a royal child. The last time that this almost barbarous tradition had been observed was at the birth of Princess Margaret. King George VI decided to end the practice, and just before Princess Elizabeth's confinement this announcement was made: 'The attendance of a Minister of the Crown at a birth in the Royal Family is not a statutory requirement or a constitutional necessity. It is merely the survival of an archaic custom, and the King feels it is unnecessary to continue further a practice for which there is no legal requirement.' So it was that Chuter Ede waited in his office for news of the birth to be telephoned through to him. Then, having filled in the missing word 'boy' on the waiting telegrams, he sent the news to governments in the Commonwealth and Empire. This boy was a prince, and a special prince too, since he was the first-born son of the King's elder daughter, a future king of England. He was the first baby born in certain succession to the throne since the birth of Prince Edward, afterwards Edward VIII and the Duke of Windsor, fifty-four years earlier.

The welcome given to the Prince's birth was world-wide. In Hyde Park and from the Tower guns boomed out their salutes, and similar salutes sounded from forts and warships all over the Commonwealth. Field-Marshal Jan Smuts, the aging Prime Minister of South Africa, cabled the King: 'We pray the prince will be a blessing to our Commonwealth and the world.' *The Washington Post* captured the feelings of many Americans: 'Now the British can sit back and relax and enjoy having "a baby in the house".' The Canadian government had an Arctic island named Prince Charles Island in honour of the Prince's birth.

The infant Prince lived the life of a normal baby if in less-than-normal surroundings. His mother breast-fed him for the first few months. He slept in the cradle which had

3

been used by his mother and his aunt Margaret when they were babies. His cot was a hundred years old, a four-poster with safety sides, last used by the King's youngest brother the Duke of Kent, who had died on wartime service when his flying boat crashed in Scotland in 1942. When, later, Charles was taken for walks out of doors, he went in a pram which had been used for his mother and his aunt. His first toy was an ivory-handled rattle given him when he was only a few hours old by a fond grandmother who had bought it for Princess Elizabeth and had kept it ever since.

But he was not only heir to antique cots, cradles, prams and toys. A descendant of Queen Victoria and of the Electress Sophia, to whom the royal family owe their claim to the throne under the Act of Settlement, he is also a descendant of James VI of Scotland who, as James I of England, united the two countries to form Great Britain. Through the Yorkist line Charles can trace his descent from William the Conqueror, although he is also a descendant of John of Gaunt, the ancestor of the Lancastrian kings. He can claim as another ancestor Alfred the Great, which, if Anglo-Saxon chronicles are to be believed, gives him a pedigree going back to the god Woden. Through Mary Queen of Scots, mother of James I, he is descended from Robert the Bruce and St Margaret of Scotland. His Welsh ancestry stems from Henry Tudor who in turn was a descendant of the great Llewellyn-ap-Gruffyd, Prince of All Wales.

Although Charles' father was born a prince of Greece, he did not have any Greek blood in his veins. Prince Philip is a member of the Danish royal house of Schleswig-Holstein-Sonderburg-Glucksburg. In 1863 the Greek people invited Prince William of Denmark (Prince Philip's grandfather) to become king of their recently independent country; he took the title of King George I. His sister became Queen Alexandra of England, wife of Edward VII. Both Charles' parents are therefore great-great-grandchildren of King Christian IX of Denmark. They are also great-great-grandchildren of Queen Victoria, whose daughter Alice married Prince Louis IV of Hesse and gave birth to two daughters. One, Alix (Alexandra), became the ill-fated wife of Nicholas II, the last tsar of Russia; the other, Victoria, married a German, Prince Louis of Battenberg (the name was later anglicized to Mountbatten). There were three children of that marriage: two boys, Prince George and Prince Louis, and a girl, Princess Alice. She married Prince Andrew of Greece and the offspring of that marriage was Prince Philip. George I of Greece was assassinated in 1913 and Philip's uncle, Constantine, succeeded to the throne only to be deposed in 1917. Constantine's son became the puppet king Alexander I, but died of blood poisoning in 1920. The Greeks invited Constantine to ascend the throne again, only to force him to abdicate for a second time in 1922. Philip's cousin, George, then

4

became King George II. His career was a very mixed one – he abdicated in 1923, was restored to the throne in 1935, expelled in 1946 and restored again in 1946.

Philip was born on the island of Corfu in 1921. When his uncle was expelled in 1922, Philip and the rest of the royal family were forced to leave the country – the infant Philip was brought out on a Royal Navy ship in a cot made of orange boxes. The young Prince of Greece was well looked after by his Mountbatten uncles, Louis and George – his education at Cheam and Gordonstoun was paid for by his uncle George, while his uncle Louis arranged for him to sit the entrance examinations for Dartmouth Naval College in 1939, where he was trained as a naval officer.

It was Lord Louis who arranged the first meeting of the two royal relations, Philip and Elizabeth, which took place at Dartmouth in July 1939. The story of their courtship, engagement and marriage has been frequently told. Before their engagement the young Prince had to become a naturalized Briton. He also had to renounce his Greek titles and all other foreign dignities. This made him, for the time being at least, a commoner. It did not solve the problem of the surname by which he was to be known. Few people in royal circles thought that he ought to use his own family name of Schleswig-Holstein-Sonderburg-Glucksburg on his newly issued British passport. The Home Secretary, Chuter Ede, suggested that the young man should associate himself with his mother's family name. Although the male members of the Battenberg family had anglicized the name to Mountbatten, Philip's mother had never done so, but Chuter Ede thought that this seemingly minor omission could be overlooked. So it was that the Danish Prince, with a Greek title and birthplace, became Lieutenant Philip Mountbatten, a name which he shared with his uncles George and Louis.

On 19 November 1947, just before his wedding to Princess Elizabeth, George VI created Philip a Knight of the Order of the Garter, gave him the style of Royal Highness, and raised him to the peerage as Baron Greenwich, Earl of Merioneth and Duke of Edinburgh. He was not given the title of Prince – perhaps, as Dermot Morrah suggests, because George VI assumed that the style of Royal Highness carried that of Prince with it. Since the father was not officially dubbed Prince, his children would not have had the titles of Prince or Princess according to the royal warrant issued by George V on 11 December 1917, which stated that:

> The children of any Sovereign of the United Kingdom, and the children of the sons of any such Sovereign, and the eldest living son of the eldest son of the Prince of Wales, shall have and at all times hold and enjoy the style, title or attribute of Royal Highness, with their titular dignity of Prince or Princess

prefixed to their respective Christian names, or with their other titles of honour. That, save as aforesaid, the titles of Royal Highness, Highness, or Serene High-ness and the titular dignity of Prince or Princess shall cease, except those titles already granted and remaining unrevoked.

To ensure that his grandchildren would be royally styled, George VI issued letters patent under the Great Seal on 9 November 1948, just before the birth of the new heir. In these the King conferred on all children born to the Duke and Duchess of Edinburgh the style of His or Her Royal Highness, and the title of Prince or Princess with a christian name. This amended the terms of George V's royal warrant by putting Princess Elizabeth on the same footing as any son of the sovereign. Thus one factor concerning the child's names and titles was settled.

There was still some uncertainty, however, about the child's surname which would, in due course, become the name of a dynasty. Over the centuries Britain has been ruled by a succession of dynasties from the Angevins to the Hanoverians, the last of whom – Victoria – married Albert of Saxe-Coburg-Gotha. In 1914 Britain went to war against Germany, and an outbreak of hysterical jingoism led to public attacks on all things German, from sausages to Beethoven. The outcry reached fever pitch in October 1914, with demands in the popular press for the resignation of the King's cousin, Prince Louis of Battenberg, from the post of First Sea Lord because, it was argued, he could not be trusted to command the Royal Navy against possible German attacks. The outcry ignored the fact that the Prince had served in the Royal Navy for forty-six years and that he had won his high rank on merit. He had been born a German, which was sufficient to condemn him in the eyes of the British press. A House of Lords committee was set up to examine the position of other foreign princes still, technically at least, members of the British royal house though married into European royal families. The committee reported in 1917, and one effect of its findings was that the Duke of Cumberland, the Duke of Brunswick and Viscount Taffe were deprived of their titles because they had 'adhered to the King's enemies' during the war. Another, and more significant, outcome of the report was that it caused George V to ask the College of Heralds what his own surname was. The College claimed that it was not sure, fearing perhaps in the patriotic days of 1917 to declare that England's king had a German-sounding name. So George V decided to take a new name; various suggestions were made – York, Lancaster, Stuart, Tudor-Stuart and Fitzroy – and rejected. Then Lord Stamfordham, a trusted secretary, discovered that Edward III had at one time been called Edward of Windsor, and on 17 July 1917 the following statement was approved for publication by the Privy Council:

Prince Charles, aged one month, with his mother at Buckingham Palace.

Charles with his Scottish nanny, Helen Lightbody.

We, of Our Royal Will and Authority, do hereby declare and announce that as from the date of this Our Royal Proclamation Our House and Family shall be styled and known as the House and Family of Windsor, and that all the descen- dants in the male line of Our said Grandmother Queen Victoria who are subjects of these Realms, other than female descendants who may marry or may have married, shall bear the said Name of Windsor.

And do hereby further declare and announce that We for Ourselves and for and on behalf of Our descendants and all other descendants of Our said Grandmother Queen Victoria who are subjects of these Realms, relinquish and enjoin the discontinuance of the use of the degrees, styles, dignities, titles and honours of Dukes and Duchesses of Saxony and Princes and Princesses of Saxe-Coburg- Gotha, and all other German degrees, styles, dignitaries, titles, honours and appellations to Us or to them heretofore belonging or appertaining.

Other members of the royal family were also invited to change their names; the Battenberg brothers became Mountbatten, taking the English titles of Marquis of Milford Haven and Marquis of Carisbrooke.

So the new Prince's mother was a Windsor, while his father was a Mountbatten, and on 15 December 1948 the birth of the young Prince Charles Mountbatten was registered by the registrar of births, marriages and deaths for the City of Westminster, within which the Palace lies. On 9 April 1952, some two months after her accession, the Queen declared her 'Will and Pleasure that She and her Children shall be styled and known as the House and Family of Windsor, and Her descendants, other than female descendants who marry, shall bear the name of Windsor.'

The registration certificate showed that the child's christian names were Charles Philip Arthur George. There was a good deal of surprise when the names had been announced about a month after his birth. The other two monarchs to bear the name Charles had both had unhappy reigns, while another Stuart, Bonnie Prince Charlie, had led a rebellion against the Hanoverian George II in 1745. Maybe the choice of name was an attempt to break with a legend; perhaps it was an early attempt to assuage Scottish national pride; more likely it was a tribute to the infant's godfather, King Haakon of Norway, who had been known as Prince Charles of Denmark until he accepted the throne of Norway in 1905. Arthur is a traditional royal name. It was used by Henry VII, the first Welsh king of England, whose heir, Arthur, died before his father and so enabled Henry VIII to come to the throne. Queen Victoria had given the name to her son, the Duke of Connaught, who had been godfather to Princess Elizabeth. That the child was called Philip after his father and George after his grandfather was not unexpected.

The infant Prince's birth was registered on the morning of 15 December. In the afternoon he was christened by Dr Fisher, the Archbishop of Canterbury, at Buckingham Palace. The Palace chapel had been wrecked by German bombs in September 1940, so the ceremony was held in the Music Room, overlooking the Palace gardens. The Lily Font, designed by Prince Albert for the baptism of Queen Victoria's first child in 1840, was brought from Windsor. Holy water from the River Jordan was used, a tradition dating from the days of the Crusades. Prince Charles wore a robe of Honiton lace over satin, which had been worn at the christenings of all Queen Victoria's children as well as by the children of George v and George vi. The godparents present were King George vi and Queen Elizabeth, Prince Philip's cousin – Lady Brabourne, and the elderly but still erect and dignified Queen Mary. Other godparents had been unable to travel; Princess Margaret and her uncle, David Bowes-Lyon, acted as proxies for the infant Prince's great-grand-uncles, King Haakon and Prince George of Greece, and for Prince Philip's mother, Princess Alice of Greece, who had been a member of a Greek religious order since becoming a widow and was therefore unable to attend.

Prince Charles spent the first few months of his life in and around Buckingham Palace. This was not his parents' official home. Before his birth they had lived in a rented house at Windlesham in Surrey while their own home, Clarence House, was being renovated. George vi had settled Clarence House on them and hoped that they would be able to live there. The house had been the home of King William iv, the Duke of Clarence, before his accession in 1830. Later it had belonged to the Duke of Connaught, who had, however, retired just after World War i to live in Bagshot. During World War ii King George vi lent the almost derelict house to the British Red Cross, who converted it into offices. When it was returned to the royal family in 1948 it was badly in need of re-conversion, modernization and decoration. Labour and materials were very scarce in the post-war years, and work on Clarence House took longer than had been expected.

When the Duke and Duchess of Edinburgh moved into their new home in July 1949 they must have welcomed the change from the rambling Palace to this modern-ized, labour-saving, centrally-heated house. The nursery suite was at the front of the building, looking across the Mall to St James's Park. Here the Scottish nanny, Miss Helen Lightbody, looked after her charge as she had looked after the sons of the Duke and Duchess of Gloucester. As her assistant she had Mabel Anderson, the Liverpool-born daughter of a policeman. 'Maba', as she became known to the growing Prince, had been chosen by Princess Elizabeth after advertising in a nursing journal and personally interviewing some of the applicants. When Helen Lightbody retired in

1956, Mabel Anderson took over the nursery and remained in charge of the other royal babies.

Nanny Lightbody and Miss Anderson ruled over the nursery quarters. The young Prince learned to walk in the day nursery, which was also the nurses' sitting-room. Here there were four armchairs and a sofa, to and from which he could toddle past a guarded fireplace. Here, too, was the glass-fronted case where his toys and picture books were kept, and the folding play pen in which, like other children, he spent much of his waking time. Nurserymaids kept the rooms tidy, and a nursery footman brought in meals. Every day the Prince was taken for a walk around the garden of the house or in St James's Park or Green Park, where few people paid much attention to what seemed to be ordinary nannies pushing an ordinary pram. Sometimes the Prince was taken to see his 'Gan-Gan' in Marlborough House, where he was given much more freedom than had been permitted to his mother and aunt when they visited Queen Mary. Charles was four and a half when the old Queen died, but he is said to have vivid memories of her sitting bolt upright in her room, surrounded by her collection of precious objects which she had gathered during her long life. There can be little doubt that the aging Queen, who would survive her husband and three of her sons, and had suffered a great deal when another son abdicated, must have been made happier in her old age by the rompings and antics of a growing prince on whom the future of the dynasty depended.

She may have compared the way in which the young Prince was being brought up with that in which she and her husband, George V, had brought up their own children. Harold Nicolson, the official biographer of George V, was compelled by all the evidence he gathered to conclude that: 'There is no doubt that King George V and Queen Mary failed in their relationships with their children and were for different reasons temperamentally unsuited to parenthood.' King George V was a strict disciplinarian who was often harsh in word and deed to his children. The Queen, says another royal biographer, 'found it difficult "to stand between them and the sudden gusts of their father's wrath"'. In his biography of the Earl of Derby, Randolph Churchill attributed to King George V a now widely quoted statement: 'My father was frightened of his mother. I was frightened of my father and I am damned well going to see to it that my children are frightened of me.' In his several autobiographical sketches Edward VIII, the Duke of Windsor, recalls the fear and eventually dislike that he felt for his father. George V had recorded Edward's birth in his diary: 'A sweet little boy was born.' Those, according to Edward, were the last kind words that his father used about him.

Prince Charles' upbringing was radically different. This can partly be explained by the nature of the relationship between his parents, which was unlike relationships between many previous occupants of the British throne. Theirs was a love match, not a political convenience, and no one can deny the truth behind the fulsome claim that 'the love of Princess Elizabeth and Prince Philip . . . ranks with the great royal romances of history.' Ample evidence can be found in memoirs, published letters and the less reliable gossipy books written by former servants that there was no 'fixing' of this marriage; that, on the contrary, King George VI kept the young couple apart as far as he was able until he was finally convinced of the genuine nature of their great affection for one another.

Princess Elizabeth had enjoyed a happy childhood with a loving father and mother who gave their children a secure, united home. It is not altogether surprising that she has given her own children the same background. She did her best to save the infant Prince from being treated as an oddity or like a film star, and she gave him that genuine affection which a child needs. As a princess she was a member of 'the royal firm', so that she was often away from home performing her royal duties. But when-ever she was at home, she showed a clear determination to fill the role of mother. After breakfast she played with Charles for an hour or so – and as far as she has been able, she has always devoted that time to her other children. She supervised some meals, especially tea, insisting that one sort of food must be finished before a cake or some other favourite was permitted. After tea there was an hour and a half during which the Princess and – if he was at home – Charles' father, played with their son. Then the parents would take the young Prince for his daily bath; Princess Elizabeth would put on a waterproof apron, and both mother and father would enjoy the splashing of an excited child playing with bath-time toys.

His mother insisted that the child should be called Charles by everyone in the nursery, rather than 'Your Royal Highness'. Princess Elizabeth had been obliged to curtsey to her 'Grandpa England' and Queen Mary; she said that there would be no formalities of this kind where her son was concerned. Charles' mother gave him his first simple lessons with the kind of picture books to be found in countless homes throughout the country; the Prince's favourite was the *Babar the Elephant* series. With the aid of building blocks she taught him his letters and, using a bead frame, his numbers. After Princess Anne was born, Charles played in the nursery while his mother sat and fed the infant Princess. At other times he toddled along when his mother or father pushed the baby in the pram around the garden of Clarence House.

Both parents always made sure that the children were properly disciplined. Charles and Anne slept on hair mattresses and pillows. They were taught to stand perfectly still for long periods, in preparation for the public ceremonies which they would one day have to attend. When they deserved it they were smacked – by father, mother or servants. On the other hand, as is normal in many families, the children tended to be spoilt by their grandparents.

Prince Philip was a naval officer. After serving for some time at the Admiralty he was sent to Malta as a lieutenant in the *Chequers*. In 1949 Princess Elizabeth spent Christmas with him, leaving Charles at Sandringham with her mother and father. When later, as Queen, she was obliged to leave her children behind with their grandmother, she did so with the confidence that both children and grandmother enjoyed each other's company. In Australia she was once asked if she did not miss the children. 'More than they miss us, I'm afraid. You see, they have a doting grandmother.'

Princess Anne was born on 15 August 1950 and Charles proved to be an affectionate, protective and proud older brother. At Christmas 1950 Princess Elizabeth flew out again to spend some time with her naval officer husband, now a lieutenantcommander in command of the destroyer *Magpie*. Once again the grandparents played their part, this time having both the infants to stay with them at Sandringham. Charles, now a sturdy twoyearold, was big enough to toddle around the house, visit the kennels and even be taken on a visit to King's Lynn to see the ships on which, he seemed to hope, he might find his father. On New Year's Day 1951 he had a very pleasant surprise when the telephone was placed in his ear – he cried out in disbelief: 'Why, it's Mummy – from *Magpie*.' It was during this holiday that he met Herbert Morrison, then Lord President of the Council, who had been summoned with others to attend a Privy Council. Morrison, hearing the patter of feet, turned to see the young Prince running along behind him, and is alleged to have said: 'Sorry, young fellermelad, but I'm afraid you can't go in there. We've got a meeting with your grandfather and it's very, very secret. Ever so secret. One day . . . well, you'll learn about that in due course.' Even if the story is not authentic, like many such tales it has a ring of truth about it. It is certainly true that the King wrote to his daughter in Malta, 'Charles is too sweet, stumping around the room. We shall love having him at Sandringham. He is the fifth generation to live there and I hope he will get to like the place.'

Unfortunately, George VI's health was steadily getting worse, and Princess Elizabeth was being called on to perform an increasing number of royal functions in his place. In July 1951 Prince Philip reluctantly had to give up command of the *Magpie* to help his wife with her work. In September the King had another operation which delayed the start of a journey which the Duke and Duchess of Edinburgh were to make to Canada. They finally set off in October, taking with them documents that Princess Elizabeth would have to sign if her father died while she was abroad.

Both she and her mother knew, although the King did not, that he had cancer.

Charles was now a three-year-old and he has vivid memories of this holiday and of his grandfather. In particular Charles remembers sitting with him on his third birthday while a photographer took a picture that was to become well known. To help keep him quiet, Richard Colville, press secretary to George VI, swung his watch, which Charles remembers only as 'something shiny'. The Queen now has this picture in her private sitting-room, in memory of her father who had such an influence on her and whom her eldest son resembles in so many ways.

Princess Elizabeth telephoned Clarence House as often as she could during this journey which took her right through Canada and, very briefly, to Washington, USA, where she met President Truman. Charles spoke to his mother and looked forward to her return and to the presents which she would bring. On 17 November Charles was taken to meet his parents on their return. It was one of his first public engagements and reporters commented on the likeness to his father – his hands stuck in his pockets or clasped firmly behind his back. Back at Sandringham he had all the excitement of examining and playing with his new toys – cowboy outfits, Indian headdresses, polar bear rugs to go beside the bed. His grandparents had the pleasure of knowing that their daughter had done another difficult job in an exceptionally fine, professional manner. On 4 December, as if in thanks to both of them for what they had done, the King had the Duke and Duchess of Edinburgh sworn in as members of the Privy Council. The young Princess and her youthful husband were to be more closely involved in the machinery of government.

The young Prince, meanwhile, was free to enjoy the process of growing up in the security of that happy atmosphere generated by grandparents, parents and servants. At Sandringham he had more freedom than he had in Clarence House. In London he and his sister were taken for walks in the royal parks, but increasingly the public began to follow the nanny pushing the pram, with the toddling Charles holding on. Sometimes he and Princess Anne were taken by car to Richmond Park or Wimbledon Common where they could play more freely, Charles pushing his favourite Jumbo which helped him to walk more steadily each day. As he became more active there were games to be played, hide-and-seek in the bracken in the parks, or football matches in which chauffeurs and detectives were invited to join. At his birth Queen Mary had remarked how like Prince Albert he looked. But as he grew into a boy of three it became clear that he had many of his father's features. Perhaps most noticeable were the prominent ears to which he now makes joking reference. He also revealed some of his mother's features, particularly around the mouth and eyes. He inherited many of the personal qualities of his grandfather, George VI. Like him he was shy, serious and patient. Like his maternal grandmother he was dignified and very thoughtful, especially where his baby sister was concerned. All in all, the royal family had every right to be pleased with the development of the young Prince.

But the happiness of that homecoming and the joys of Christmas 1951 seemed very distant when Charles learned that his mother and father were soon to set out on yet another tour, this time to Australia and New Zealand. Charles and Anne remained at Sandringham on 31 January 1952 when the King and Queen went to London Airport to see the young parents off on their long journey. The picture of the haggard and lonely-looking King waving to the aeroplane as it took off served to remind the public that their monarch was indeed a sick man. The Duke and Duchess stopped off in Africa, at the hunting lodge on the Sagana River which the people of Kenya had given them as a wedding present. On 5 February they stayed the night at Treetops, a little cabin in a huge fir tree overlooking a water hole. Back in Sandringham the King had spent the day out shooting. Queen Elizabeth and Princess Margaret were out visiting the artist, Edward Seago, on the other side of Norfolk. In the early evening the King had tea and a rest and went, for the first time ever, to visit the children's nursery. He sat with them while they had supper, helped to tuck them into bed and said a prayer with them before saying goodnight. Then he went downstairs where he dined with his wife and daughter on their return. Sometime that night he died in his sleep.

His valet discovered that he was dead when he failed to wake him for his morning bath at 7.30 on 6 February. The Queen, in spite of her own sorrow, was determined that 'their lives must not be affected by what has happened.' But the death of a very popular King could not be completely hidden from the children who watched as servants came and went, many crying as they did so. At 4.30, when it was time for tea, the children were not taken to have it with Granny but in their nursery, where Helen Lightbody, at the request of Queen Elizabeth, explained to three-year-old Charles that his grandfather had 'gone away'. Later the puzzled Charles demanded to see his granny who came to tell him that 'Mummy and Papa will soon be home.' Charles asked, in that persistent way he has shown since, many questions natural in the circumstances. Where had Grandpa gone? Why so quickly? Why hadn't he said goodbye? The Queen could only hug her grandson in an effort to hide her grief. With his innate kindness the child patted her hand and said, 'Don't cry, Granny.'

Meanwhile, in the harsh world outside the nursery, life went relentlessly on. The blinds were drawn in Buckingham Palace, the news of the King's death announced at a quarter to eleven, and from 11.50 the bell of St Paul's began to toll continuously for the next two hours. At five o'clock the Accession Council met at St James's Palace and declared that Princess Elizabeth was the new sovereign. At seven o'clock in the evening the members of both Houses of Parliament began to take their oaths of allegiance to the new monarch.

News of the King's death had been telephoned through to the offices of the *East African Standard*, in Nairobi. It was a reporter on that paper who telephoned the Princess' private secretary to tell him the news; he rang from the hotel across the valley to the hunting lodge where Michael Parker answered the telephone. Parker tried to get confirmation from the governor in Nairobi, but he had left to meet the Princess on her arrival at the next stop, Mombasa. Parker managed to pick up a BBC programme, and although he did not hear a news bulletin, he realized from the solemn music being played that the report of the King's death was true. He then went to get Prince Philip from the sitting-room of the hunting lodge where, at 2.45 pm local time, the Prince was sitting with his wife. It was the Duke who broke the news to her; immediately and professionally she turned her attention to her new post. She ordered telegrams to be sent to the countries she would now be unable to visit, instructed that the Privy Council should meet as soon as she had been declared Queen by the Accession Council, and announced that she would take the title of Elizabeth II. Meanwhile, Prince Philip was organizing the quickest flight back to London. The new Queen Mother told Charles and Anne that their parents would be coming home on the following day; for Charles, the day was one of great confusion – he was excited at the thought of being with his parents again so soon, but also puzzled about the 'going away' of his friendly grandfather and the evident grief of his granny of whom he was so fond.

For the new Queen it was a sudden end to the life she had hoped to lead for some years as wife to a serving officer in the Royal Navy and mother to growing children. George VI was only fifty-nine when he died. His daughter may have hoped that he would live to the biblical three score years and ten – George V had been seventy-one when he died and the former Edward VIII was to be seventy-nine when he died in 1972. The death of George VI at a relatively early age brought the twenty-six-year-old Elizabeth to the throne some ten or twenty years sooner than she might have expected.

2
The Young
Duke of Cornwall
1952-6

The three-year-old Charles met his mother at Clarence House on the evening of 7 February 1952 where, waiting to meet the new monarch, was Queen Mary who remembered Victoria reigning gloriously and now wanted to provide some encouragement to the new, very young Queen Elizabeth II, so unexpectedly brought to the throne. Charles may have noticed that as his mother arrived at Clarence House the royal banner was run up on the flagstaff, an outward sign of the changes that would take place in the lives of the royal family.

On the following morning, the accession of the new Queen was formally proclaimed by the various Kings of Arms at St James's Palace, at Charing Cross, on the steps of the Royal Exchange in the City and at the Mercat Cross in Edinburgh. Charles would not have heard the sonorous pronouncement from nearby Friary Court in St James's Palace:

> *We do now hereby with one voice and Consent to Tongue and Heart publish and proclaim that the High and Mighty Princess Elizabeth Alexandra Mary is now, by the Death of our late Sovereign of Happy Memory, become Queen Elizabeth the Second, by the Grace of God Queen of this Realm and of all Her other Realms and Territories, Head of the Commonwealth, Defender of the Faith, to whom her lieges do acknowledge all Faith and constant Obedience, with hearty and humble Affection; beseeching God, by whom Kings and Queens do reign, to bless the Royal Princess Elizabeth the Second with long and happy Years to reign over us.*

But he may well have heard the band playing the national anthem, now to be known as *God Save the Queen*. He would have heard the boom of the forty-one-gun salute that rang out across Hyde Park, and looking from the windows of Clarence House may well have remarked on the fact that all the flags were flying lower than usual.

For Charles these things meant little, for his life went on much as it had done before. Indeed, one small but significant change was an indication of the way in which the new Queen would present her people with a new-style, 'public' monarchy. Charles and Anne had always bowed at the door before entering a room where George VI or his Queen were sitting. Queen Mary had always insisted on the need for 'majesty' to retain its dignity even under its own family roof. Queen Elizabeth, now the Queen Mother, had persuaded George VI that he had to retain that unbending dignity – hence the bowing by the royal children to the 'majesty' of the King and Queen. The new Queen decided that while this courtesy would still be shown by her children to Queen Mary and the Queen Mother, there was to be no such formal barrier between her and her children.

Charles was too young to appreciate that, as the son of the monarch, he automatically became Duke of Cornwall. Until 1337 Cornwall had been an earldom; in 1140 it had been granted to Richard, the younger brother of Henry III. In 1337 Edward III replaced the old Saxon title of earl with the French one of duke, and gave the dukedom of Cornwall to his eldest son, popularly remembered as the Black Prince, and to 'the eldest sons of his heirs being Kings of England'. Although no sovereign since 1688 has been heir to the Black Prince, this charter is still operative and, as the eldest son of the ruling sovereign, Charles became the Duke of Cornwall at the tender age of three and a half.

As Duke of Cornwall, Charles is owner of 26,000 acres in that county, including some well-known castles at Launceston, Trematon, Tintagel, Restormel, Liskeard and Maiden. He also owns 100,000 acres in Devon, Dorset, Somerset, Wiltshire, Berkshire and counties bordering on London. Included in his property is Kennington Oval in London, where Surrey and England cricketers play. At the other end of the scale is the prison at Princetown, which stands on part of the 69,000 acres of Dartmoor owned by the duchy.

The duchy brings in a large income yearly. When Princess Elizabeth was heir to the throne the income went to her father. Some of it was ploughed back into estate development which has made the duchy even more profitable. In 1953 the income was about £112,000 a year. But until Charles came of age he was entitled, under the Civil List Act of 1952, to an annual income of one-ninth of the revenue from the duchy. This money was set aside to provide for his education and to build up a fund which enabled him, later on, to employ a staff of his own.

During the winter of 1952–3 the Queen and her family continued to live at Clarence House, while Queen Elizabeth the Queen Mother and Princess Margaret lived at

Buckingham Palace, and Queen Mary resided at nearby Marlborough House. Charles did not go to George VI's funeral, and since the cortege would be passing Clarence House, he and Anne were taken to Sandringham for a short holiday. During the Easter holiday of 1953 the royal family went to stay at Windsor as had been customary for many years. Here, as at Clarence House, the young Queen gave as much time as she could to her two children, continuing her habit of playing with them after tea and of bathing them each evening whenever possible.

On their return from Windsor Charles found himself in a new home. During the holiday the Queen Mother and Princess Margaret had moved to Clarence House and the Queen, Prince Philip and the two royal children would now live at Buckingham Palace. Here the nursery apartment was six or so rooms on the third floor, looking out on to Constitution Hill and, from another set of windows, the Palace forecourt where the children watched the changing of the guard. Charles and Anne spent much of their time in a day nursery; at night Nanny Lightbody had Princess Anne in her room while Maba looked after Prince Charles.

In the main nursery the children had their toys, books, bricks, pencils, crayons and paints. On the walls were oil paintings reflecting their father's interest in the sea – a naval scene, a view of Newhaven harbour, a Tasmanian landscape and the famous *Drake's Drum*. Photographs of the children's parents and of their great-grandmother stood on the mantelpiece over the marble fireplace, alongside a cuckoo clock. Glass cases held collections of glass and china animals and other knick-knacks, among which was a miniature coffee set once owned by the Queen and her sister. Other toys and fluffy animals were to be found in the children's bedrooms, including Charles' fort with its soldiers, and Anne's dolls. More valuable dolls were kept in cases on the landing outside. These were some of the gifts which the Queen had received on her visits abroad and had brought back for the children. Here, too, were larger toys–too big to be brought into the nursery – many of them being push-along toys, others horse-drawn. There was also Charles' tricycle which he was allowed to ride in Richmond Park.

The new nursery was, as far as possible, a replica of the rooms at Clarence House, an attempt by the Queen to give her children a sense of continuity in their lives. But the young Prince was intrigued by his new home with its 620 rooms and miles of long corridors, all of which he would have liked to explore. In fact his 'voyages' were generally confined to the nursery floor and to the area around his parents' private living quarters on the floor immediately below. People remember that he always seemed to be running, with the royal corgis in tow and, later, with a small sister shouting: 'Wait for me, Charles. . . .' From the front window of the nursery he and Anne could watch parades and bands, people arriving for official receptions, and

The Queen plays with Anne and Charles at Balmoral Castle where the Royal Family spent many happy holidays.

ambassadors driving up in horse-drawn carriages to present their credentials to the Queen. During weekends in Windsor there were other, new, areas to be explored by the inquisitive Charles. It was at Windsor that, having escaped from his nanny's supervision at about 6.30 in the morning, he came across servants making tea for the other staff. He joined in and surprised one member of staff by tapping at his bedroom door and announcing, 'I've brought you your tea.'

After her accession, the Queen ensured that, as far as possible, her children were shielded from publicity, and not allowed to see newspapers containing their pictures. Sometimes they were smacked, usually by Prince Philip, who is supposed to have spanked Charles for making a face at a crowd of people, and Anne for creating a great fuss over some clothes did she not want to wear. The parents insisted that Charles and Anne behave politely to everyone. They were taught to say 'please' and 'thank you', and the easy-tempered Charles taught the more rumbustious Anne some of these lessons. At the end of one long railway journey he took her firmly by the hand along the platform towards the front of the train and was heard to say: 'Come along, Anne. We have to say "Thank you" to the engine driver.' But when Charles forgot himself and addressed a detective by his surname alone, the Queen spoke sharply to him and sent him off to 'mister' the no doubt embarrassed man.

The children were trained to do things for themselves rather than expect other people to do things for them. On one occasion Charles came into a room and left the door open. A servant went to close it. Philip ordered, 'Leave it alone, man. He's got hands. Let him do it himself.' And Charles was sent to close the door. But this was not the harsh world of the court of George V and Queen Mary – although the children were forbidden to go to the Queen's sitting-room, which was also her study where she did some of her official work, at least during her working hours. This rule has been relaxed for the two younger princes, by a mother who is herself now more relaxed in her attitude towards her work.

But apart from the restrictions imposed on her by her work, the Queen spent as much time as she could with the growing Charles and Anne. Every morning they went to see her after breakfast and the children ran to greet their royal mother with a hug and a kiss. The Queen would often spend lunchtime in the nursery and after tea the children came downstairs to be with their mother. She even got the Prime Minister to change the time of his regular Tuesday visit to fit in with the children's timetable – the report on government business had to wait until the children had been put to bed. On fine afternoons the children and their mother would play in the Palace garden with its sandpit, climbing frame and swings. Here, too, the children brought their pet animals – Charles had a rabbit called Harvey. If they had played in the garden, tea became an outdoor picnic. If they had to stay indoors, they played in the Queen's sitting-room, where she continued to help Charles with his lessons in reading, writing and arithmetic. When Prince Philip was home there was rougher play – football in the garden or along the nursery corridor, with royal corgis joining in the fun. Charles admired his athletic father who taught him to swim in the indoor pool at the rear of the Palace. This after-tea lesson was given by Michael Parker if the Prince was not free on any particular day.

When it was time for bed the Queen would take the children back to the nursery, giving a hand with the bathing which was always a more rollicking affair if the young father was at home. Servants reckoned that the noise could be heard 'all over the Palace' – which had once been described as 'a morgue' by the fun-loving but repressed Edward VII. It is not surprising that Charles believes that he had a happy childhood, and that people who watched him grow in those early years were ready in their praise for his development.

Soon after Charles' fourth birthday, preparations began for the Queen's coronation which was to take place on 2 June 1953. Charles first became aware of it when he was wandering around the Palace and found some servants brushing the long, heavy, purple robe which the Queen was to wear for part of the ceremony. He asked what they were doing and was puzzled when told that they were preparing 'the Queen's robe'. The inquisitive four-year-old asked, 'Who is the Queen?' We can't be sure that he understood the implications of the answer: 'Why, your Mummy of course.'

From his nursery window he watched the men building the wooden stands along the Mall and the troops rehearsing their part in the pageant. He saw the Prime Minister, Winston Churchill, coming and going – eager to play his rightful role in the coronation of the young Queen for whom he had a high regard and almost grandfatherly concern. Upstairs in the nursery Charles and Anne roped in the nannies and servants to play at coronations. But, downstairs, the Queen decided that although he was the senior royal duke and, as such, the head of the peerage, her young son would not be allowed to kneel before her in the Abbey to take the oath of allegiance, for she wished to protect him from the glare of publicity.

On the morning of the coronation the children were woken by the noise of trumpets and bugles and the sound of crowds gathering around the Palace. The weather was dull, overcast and threatening, with banks of clouds sweeping over London. Throughout the day there were to be heavy and frequent showers. When Charles had finished breakfast he was dressed in a frilled shirt and short, white silk trousers. His unruly hair was slicked down with hair oil in the hope that it would stay in place. From the nursery windows he watched the mile-long procession move out of Palace Yard, around the Victoria Memorial, along the Mall towards Admiralty Arch. He saw his beautifully robed mother and father riding in the royal state coach made for George III. Pulled at about three miles per hour by eight Windsor greys, the four-and-a-half-ton golden coach seemed fit for a fairy queen.

When the coach had passed into the Mall, Charles was taken by Nanny Lightbody down to a side door. Then, in a plain car, they were driven to the Abbey by a side route. They went in by a private door at the rear, Charles holding hands with Nanny Lightbody and a Coldstream Guards officer. He was taken to the front row of the royal box where he stood on a footstool between his grandmother and aunt Margaret. When he arrived, the ceremony had been going on for some time. His mother had been divested of her splendid robes and was dressed in the simplest possible white garment. She was seated in the coronation chair; four Knights of the Garter, dressed in all the finery of their blue velvet cloaks, held over her a canopy of cloth of gold. The Archbishop of Canterbury was dipping his thumb into the holy oil with which he would anoint her hands, breast and the crown of her head. Charles looked anxiously at his mother in her unaccustomed clothing, surrounded by all the men in their robes, facing the Archbishop who was in the act of raising his hand to the Queen. Just at that moment the young Queen looked across to the royal box, saw Charles, realized perhaps that he might be more than puzzled by what was going on, and gave him a smile to tell him that everything was all right.

Charles, reassured as his mother's coronation proceeded, was then seen to wipe his hands across his brilliantined hair and to offer his hands to his granny. Lip readers allege that he said, 'Granny, doesn't it smell nice?' We don't know what the Queen Mother said. We do know that she pulled him back as he leaned forward over the balcony to get a better view of the proceedings, and that he was allowed to stay longer than had first been thought desirable. His granny explained to him what was happening. When the long process of the swearing of allegiance began, Nanny Lightbody stepped in to take him back to the Palace for lunch. After the newly crowned Queen had finally returned to the Palace, she went out on to the balcony to greet the crowds and, when she had been alone for a brief moment, the children were led out by Prince Philip to join her. Here for the first time Charles became aware of the great public and its regard for the monarchy. Here for the first time he saw the vast crowds, and heard the welcoming roar for his mother, dressed like a fairy-tale, picture-book queen.

But after the drama and pageantry of the coronation it was soon back to normal for the young Prince. As part of the coronation duties the Queen and Prince Philip

Miss Peebles, nicknamed 'Misspee' by her charges, taking Anne and Charles out for a walk. She was Charles' private tutor until he started school at the age of eight.

Prince Charles tackles the high jump on sports day at his first school, Hill House. The Queen was there to watch him.

were to undertake a long tour, which was to start in November, just after Charles' fifth birthday, and last for six months. To ensure that the children did not fret too much at this long separation and that Charles' education should continue in her absence, the Queen decided to appoint a royal tutor to supervise his studies. She broke with tradition by appointing a woman, Miss Peebles, who had already been governess to the youngest son of the widowed Duchess of Kent, and a companion to his sister, Princess Alexandra. One of the rooms in the nursery block was fitted out with a small desk and a blackboard, and Miss Peebles, or 'Misspee' as the children learned to call her, took up her duties. She had a pupil whom she learned to like because he was sensible and maturely responsible – evidence of the way in which his parents had brought him up. He was also able to write, read and count because of the lessons his mother had given him. Miss Peebles found that Charles had a great sense of fun and was a quiet chuckler. With Misspee, Charles settled down to a regular timetable which, like most small children's timetables, consisted mainly of reading and writing, which he liked, and arithmetic, which he disliked. His first geography lessons were based on the royal tour which took his parents through Bermuda, Jamaica, Fiji and Tonga, on to New Zealand and Australia and home again via Ceylon and Africa.

His day began at half past nine with a bible story, as does the school day for most children. Like them, too, he learned to enjoy painting and drawing, which he did in the afternoons. Misspee took him for walks in Green Park and St James's Park, and followed up those walks by asking Charles to tell her what he had seen that interested him. His history lessons were based on a series of stories about children in history. Most of the children whose lives he studied were royal, so that, imperceptibly, he was to learn something about his own role. When Charles was six, Misspee added French to the curriculum, and took him on more educational visits – to the Science and Natural History Museums, Madame Tussaud's and the nearby planetarium. In the hope that the press and public would not interfere with this programme, the Queen's press secretary, Richard Colville, issued a letter to the press on 11 April 1955:

> *I am commanded by the Queen to say that Her Majesty and the Duke of Edinburgh have decided that their son has reached the stage when he should take part in more grown-up educational pursuits with other children.*
>
> *In consequence, a certain amount of the Duke of Cornwall's instruction will take place outside his home; for example, he will visit museums and other places of interest. The Queen trusts, therefore, that His Royal Highness will be able to enjoy this in the same way as other children without the embarrassment of constant publicity. In this respect, Her Majesty feels that it is equally important*

While their parents were away the two children spent part of their time with their granny. Weekends were spent with her at Windsor, where they played in the famous thatched cottage which the Welsh people had given to the Queen when she was six. At Windsor, Charles helped the Queen Mother with one of her favourite hobbies, gardening. With a small wheelbarrow and a set of miniature gardening tools he set about helping granny, who loved pottering about in old clothes and a floppy felt hat. The Christmas holidays were spent at Sandringham, and the excitement was heightened by the thrill of opening the parcels that the Queen and Prince Philip had left behind before setting out on their tour. And Christmas morning, 1953, was made memorable by the telephone call from 'Mummy and Papa', so many thousands of miles away in New Zealand.

Meanwhile at Buckingham Palace, Windsor and Sandringham, Misspee continued to supervise Charles' education, insisting, as his parents would have, on discipline. She once said: 'Children have to be made to realize that they cannot always have their own way.' But the admirable tutor also followed the best of the newer trends in child development. She encouraged Charles whenever she thought he was able to do more or better, but she did not push him in those subjects, such as arithmetic, which he did not like. She believed that it was essential to treat him as an individual with certain abilities and certain weaknesses. She encouraged his love for animals. Charles was the proud owner not only of his pet rabbit, but of two corgis, a hamster, and two love birds which he named David and Annie. The children were allowed to have the birds in the nursery but had to clean out the cage themselves. Their nanny, Miss Anderson, alleged that she was terrified of the birds, which she described as 'horrid, vicious creatures'. When the cage was being cleaned out the birds were free to fly around the room; Miss Anderson was terrified that, like bats, they would get entangled in her hair! Charles also had dancing lessons – his teacher was Miss Vacani from a famous London dancing school. She came to the Palace to instruct a class of young children whose parents were members of the household staff. Charles showed himself to have a natural rhythm and ability as a dancer, a foretaste of that talent he has since shown as a musician.

During the long period of separation from his parents Charles worked at his lessons, enjoyed his holidays, grew a little and became more confident and rather less shy. He looked forward eagerly to a special treat that had been promised the two children – that they could travel on *Britannia* to meet their parents at Tobruk and then sail home with them. On 15 April the children were driven to Portsmouth with the Queen Mother, who was to see them off, together with Nannies Lightbody and Anderson, and Misspee, all of whom were to go with the children. Although there was a supply of toys aboard the royal yacht, Charles insisted on taking his tricycle and pedal car; Anne took her tricycle, a dolls' house and a selection of dolls.

After an uneasy first day at sea – during which Charles was seasick – the children enjoyed themselves on board *Britannia*, where the sailors seemed to take pleasure in helping them escape from the attentions of nannies and tutor. On 22 April they arrived at Malta where their great-uncle, Lord Mountbatten, was commander-in-chief. They spent two days with him on the island, the commander taking great pride in showing Charles some of the historic places where, for example, Knights Hospitallers had defended the island during the great siege of 1551–65 when it was under attack by the Turks.

The *Britannia* then sailed to Tobruk where, on 2 May, the Queen was ceremoniously piped aboard and, after six long months, reunited with her children. Charles had watched as the officers and men lined up to greet the Queen, who shook hands with most of them. He lined up at the end and held out his hand. The Queen was heard to say: 'Not you, darling,' as she guided him into her private drawing-room for a private reunion. From Tobruk the *Britannia* sailed to Malta and Gibraltar, where they spent a few days of pleasant relaxation. Then the yacht returned to London, where Charles walked behind his parents to the reception at Westminster pier, and sat with them as they were driven back through the cheering crowds to the Palace.

Once again, it was away from the drama and pageantry, back to reality. After Mummy's half hour with the children, lessons started at 9.30 and went on until eleven. Then followed an outing – to a museum, one of London's famous streets or landmarks or through one of the parks. Once again there was reading and writing and – unfortunately – arithmetic. In the afternoons other children were invited to join in games and play at the Palace, or at Windsor when the family were there; they were also invited to take holidays with the family at Balmoral and Sandringham. There were official ceremonies such as Trooping the Colour, which Charles watched with his granny from one of the balconies overlooking Horseguards Parade. From a loft in St George's Chapel, Windsor, he watched the annual service of the Knights of the Garter, with Sir Winston Churchill, most recently appointed of the Knights, bringing up the rear. In that sense Charles was not an ordinary boy, nor could we expect

With his great-uncle, Lord Mountbatten, in Malta, where the latter was Commander-in-Chief. He was looking after Anne and Charles before they were reunited with their parents in Tobruk after a long separation.

him to be so. But he was like other small boys in many other ways. He learned to play cricket (summer 1956) and football (winter 1956), but never really enjoyed either. He much preferred swimming, an interest he shares with both his father and mother. Charles first saw table tennis being played in the servants' quarters at Balmoral and learned the game there, grubbing around on the floor of the servants' hall to get the ball when it went under a table or sideboard. At Balmoral, too, he could go on picnics on the heather-covered hills, often with his German cousins, the children of Prince Philip's sister who had married Prince George of Hanover. The eldest son was a year older than Charles, another was a year younger and the sister was about three years older than Princess Anne. Charles also learned how to ride a bicycle, which could be used when the royal parents drove off to a picnic spot – Charles, and later Anne, would follow on their bikes. There were barbecues, and overnight expeditions with an adventurous and popular father who loved to take his children swimming, fishing and cooking before settling down to spend the night in sleeping bags in some distant shooting lodge.

At Sandringham Charles had other opportunities – to shoot, and to explore the large estate which has its own fire station and which Charles made a favourite play-place. Here he was allowed to put on a fireman's helmet, sit in the driver's seat and act out the part enjoyed by countless other young boys. Christmas was spent at Sandringham and sometimes it snowed. Nanny, father and children all helped to build a snowman in front of the house so that they could see it from the nursery window. The royal parents would join with the children in snowball fights. One morning Prince Philip came out of the main door to find Charles throwing snow-balls at a policeman solemnly beating his way on guard around the house. The policeman was not sure what he ought to do. The father shouted: 'Don't just stand there, man. Throw some back.' Is there in retirement some former policeman who regales his grandchildren with the story of how he pelted the future monarch?

3
The Young Schoolboy
1956-61

In the autumn of 1956, when Charles was almost eight, the Queen made a very important and tradition-breaking decision concerning the future education of her son and our future King. Queen Victoria's sons had all been educated at home by male tutors until they were old enough, in the case of the Prince of Wales, to go to Cambridge University. This pattern had been followed for Edward VII's sons; they had their private tutors with them even when the future Edward VIII and George VI went to Dartmouth Naval College and to university. During her own childhood the Queen was brought up by a governess, Miss Crawford, who was to make a great deal of money out of many columns of print in which she related the details of life with the little Princesses. The Queen had also had a series of private tutors, including the Provost of Eton, the historian Sir Henry Marten. One of his main functions was to teach constitutional history to the heir-apparent. But she had no contact with people outside the Palace until 1944 when she persuaded her father, George VI, to let her join the ATS where she underwent the normal training as 'Second Subaltern Elizabeth Alexandra Mary Windsor, age eighteen'.

We cannot know whether, as a mother, the Queen remembered the loneliness and isolation of her upbringing in the Palace, through whose railings she could see, but not meet, people in the world outside. We can be sure that she was influenced by the ideas of her husband, whose own upbringing had been very different from hers. He was only eighteen months old when he was rescued from Greece. At six he went to an American kindergarten in St Cloud in Paris, where the majority of pupils were children of American businessmen and diplomats, so that Prince Philip learned to speak English with a slight American accent. When he left, he became a boarder at Cheam School in Surrey. His sister, Theodora, was married to Berthold, the son of Prince Max of Baden who had founded a new type of school at Salem in Germany. Berthold was headmaster of the school, and when Philip left Cheam he was sent to

Salem, where the main aim was to train boys for leadership through teaching them to serve other people. After a year there the young Philip had earned a reputation for mocking the Nazi government, comparing the Nazi salute to raising one's hand to ask permission to leave the classroom to go to the toilet. So he was transferred to Gordonstoun, a Salem-type school in Scotland. Philip's own education seemed to him to offer the best of all possible worlds. He summed up his ideas on the subject like this: 'The art of education is to combine formal training with as wide a variety of experiences as possible including some which involve a calculated risk. I think education is intended to produce intelligent, morally strong, self-sufficient human beings willing and capable of improving the machinery of living which man has created for his enjoyment.' He understands that there is no need for a future king to be a brilliant academic; indeed, there might well be dangers in having too bright a king. Not for nothing was James I known as the wisest fool in Christendom.

During a visit to the USA in 1956 Prince Philip issued a statement in which he declared: 'The Queen and I want Charles to go to school with other boys of his generation and to learn to live with other children and to absorb from childhood the discipline imposed by education with others.' This was, indeed, a break with tradition. It was something which many pundits and columnists, politicians and commentators had been advocating for a year or so. They had also, incidentally, been busy drawing up short-lists of people to whom the eight-year-old might become engaged. The fact that, universally, they were wrong about the future queen has not prevented them from pontificating on innumerable occasions since. Some advocated that Charles should be sent to the nearest primary school; others that he attend some village school. The publicity-seeking Lord Altrincham, leader of the attack on the monarchy in 1957, wrote:

> But will she have the wisdom to give her children an education very different from her own? Will she, above all, see to it that Prince Charles is equipped with all the knowledge he can absorb without injury to his health, and that he mixes during his formative years with children who will one day be bus-drivers, dockers, engineers, etc, not merely with future landowners or stockbrokers?

It takes little consideration to see that there was a good deal to recommend the idea that the future King should mix with his subjects. It took equally little time to see that the choice of school posed more problems than seemed to have occurred to Altrincham and the rest. The Queen had personally advertised for a nanny for her son, and had interviewed a number before selecting the admirable Miss Anderson. She had also made a personal choice when she appointed Misspee to supervise the Prince's first steps along the educational road. And it was once again the Queen who,

The Queen and Prince Philip smile at Charles and Anne playing happily on a
see-saw which they found in the grounds of a sawmill on the Balmoral estate.

From an early age, Charles had to get used to the glare of publicity. Here the royal
children are accompanying their mother on a visit to the famous Braemar Games.

with Prince Philip, made the decision to send Charles to a day school and who chose the school he would attend.

In October 1956 she invited Colonel Townend, the founder and then head-master of Hill House School in Hans Place, Knightsbridge, to tea at the Palace, and asked him to take her son as a pupil. Colonel Townend had founded the school in 1952. Most of the boys started at the age of five and were the sons of professional people living in the area – doctors, officers in the army or navy, MPs, journalists, lawyers and diplomats. When Charles started at the school one of the pupils was a grandson of Harold Macmillan – then Chancellor of the Exchequer, but soon to become Prime Minister in the aftermath of the Suez debacle and Sir Anthony Eden's resignation.

One of the reasons why the Queen liked this school in particular was that about one third of the boys were sons of foreign diplomats, so that Charles would be meeting boys from many different countries. Prince Philip is said to have been impressed by the sense of order and discipline which permeated the school, where all the male teachers wore blazers, white shirts and flannel trousers and the boys were equally smartly uniformed. The pupils were taught in groups of eight or nine, and Colonel Townend insisted on a high standard of work from everyone.

While Colonel Townend must have been flattered that his school had been chosen, he no doubt feared that the publicity hounds of the popular press might well make the Prince's stay at the school almost intolerable and have a bad effect on the education of the rest of the boys. For this reason it was decided that the Prince should attend school only in the afternoons for the remainder of the Michaelmas term. He had lessons with Misspee in the Palace in the morning, after which he would be taken to Hill House to join in games. In spite of every attempt to keep the secret, photographers and reporters were thick on the ground around Hill House on the afternoon of 7 November 1956 when Prince Charles stepped from a car and ran into the school. For the rest of that term the Prince was taken to Hill House every afternoon, to change from his school uniform into the shorts and sweaters that everyone else was wearing. Then, somewhere in the line of boys, he walked across the King's Road to the grounds of the Duke of York's Headquarters where the boys played football and did athletics. Perhaps because it was the first time that he had been involved in the hurly-burly that goes on under the name of boys' football, the Prince showed little enthusiasm or spirit, although he had no choice but to attend and play.

It was decided that Prince Charles would become a full-time pupil at the school from the start of the spring term. Misspee had taught him so well that Charles' marks in his pre-school test showed that he was well able to join the boys in form six of the middle school. Once he started at Hill House, Misspee would be free to concentrate on Princess Anne's education. Meanwhile, with Prince Philip away during the winter of 1956–7 at the Melbourne Olympics and on a visit to Antarctica, the Queen decided that the growing Charles needed a male tutor. During the Christmas holidays the headmaster of St Peter's School, Seaford, was invited to stay at Sandringham and to act as Charles' tutor. In this way he was, as it were, weaned from the gentler methods of Misspee and gradually introduced into a world where most of his teachers would be men.

On 28 January 1957 Prince Charles was registered as a fulltime pupil at Hill House. He started to study Latin under the headmaster, who also coached him and the other boys at games. This is hardly surprising, for Colonel Townend was an Oxford soccer blue, had been president of the university athletic club and a member of the British team at the Empire Games, and was an outstanding skirunner. Mrs Townend, a qualified nurse, taught elementary anatomy and showed the Prince how to administer artificial respiration. His first school report showed that he enjoyed history, art and french, was a very good reader and writer, was 'good' at geography and gymnastics, but was below average for arithmetic on which he was 'not very keen'. His parents were delighted with the way in which he overcame his natural shyness and got on with the unroyal business of going to school with other boys. At the Palace he was given a bedroom of his own, his nanny was replaced by a nurse 'in charge of the children's quarters', and the young Prince was seen to be growing not only physically, but also in selfconfidence.

During a visit to the Royal Tournament of 1957 Prince Charles was very excited by the activities of the teams in the gun display. He persuaded Colonel Townend that the boys in his class should be allowed to practise this difficult task and, if they succeeded, put on a show for the parents at the sports day, known at Hill House as Field Day. The Prince and his friends made their own wooden gun barrel, about seven feet long, with wheels about three feet in diameter and a plasterboard gunshield. On the field at Chelsea they practised unloading the gun, taking it apart, swinging it piece by piece across a ditch ten feet wide and reassembling it before coming to attention. There was no real ditch, so they had created one out of a wooden corridor. On Field Day, Charles' friends did their piece, his sister Anne joining in the applause, while across the field rang the voice of the proud father, 'Well done, Charles'. Later, after a game of cricket and some races, Charles was allowed to present his team to his mother, father and sister. It is little wonder that most of them remember him as 'a good chap'.

In the summer term he learned cricket but failed to shine at this very English game. He was much happier when, during the summer holidays of 1957, he went sailing on Prince Philip's yacht *Bluebottle* at Cowes, and, after the first race, was allowed to take

33

the helm. He enjoyed the easy way in which his father and the rest of the people in the crew accepted him as a crew member. He also liked sharing his father's interests – as a former naval officer Prince Philip maintained his connections with the sea. Even though Charles suffered from seasickness he insisted on sailing as often as he could.

During 1957 there was a wave of attacks upon the monarchy. Lord Altrincham, the editor and owner of the *National and English Review*, produced an edition of the *Review* in 1957 devoted almost entirely to the question of monarchy. Most of the articles were written by people who had nothing but praise for monarchy and monarchs; it was Altrincham's own contribution which caught the attention of the press and commentators, eager for headlines during the 'silly season' of August. Altrincham attacked the Queen herself:

> *Like her mother she appears to be unable to string even a few sentences together without a written text. When she has lost the bloom of youth, the Queen's reputation will depend, far more than it does now, upon her personality. It will not then be enough for her to go through the motions; she will have to say things which people can remember and do things on her own initiative which will make people sit up and take notice. As yet there is little sign that such a personality is emerging.*

Daily and Sunday newspapers took up the theme; some became staunch defenders of the monarch, while others joined in the easy task of monarch-baiting. Malcolm Muggeridge wrote a long article for the *Saturday Evening Post* in which he condemned what he called the 'royal soap opera'. The playwright John Osborne, then going through his angry young man phase, wrote in October 1957: 'It bores me, it distresses me that there should be so many empty minds, so many empty lives in Britain to sustain this fatuous industry. My objection to the royal symbol is that it is dead; it is a gold filling in a mouth full of decay. When the mobs rush forward in the Mall they are taking part in the last circus of a civilization that has lost faith in itself and sold itself for a splendid triviality.' These, and others, used the opportunity to condemn the monarch for being out of touch with the modern idiom, and for being responsible for Britain's failure to become as industrialized, modernized and successful as the USA, Germany, Japan and other industrial nations.

Fortunately for the young Prince these controversies made little difference to his way of life, whether at Hill House or at home, wherever that might be. During termtime he lived at the Palace where he continued to enjoy the security provided by a young mother who liked being with him and his sister. While they had to take lessons with Misspee, at least until Christmas, there were also card games, model cars, trains, painting, riding, swimming and charades. They spent weekends at Windsor, and longer holidays there or at Sandringham, Balmoral or one of the other royal estates, where Charles could enjoy the company of his young relations as well as that of the young children of the Queen's own friends.

Even while Lord Altrincham was preparing his broadside on the monarchy, the Queen and Prince Philip were preparing the announcement of what, in their terms, was quite an attack on royal tradition. While Charles was at Hill House during the spring and summer of 1957 his parents had given considerable thought to the next stage in his education. Having once decided that Charles was to be educated with other children, it became obvious that they had committed themselves to sending him to some sort of secondary school where he would prepare for university like other boys of his age. While Altrincham and other former Etonians advocated that he would be best off in a state secondary school, others argued that Eton or Harrow or another leading public school would provide the best training for him. But that decision would not have to be made until he was a little older and, while the Queen was anxious to break with the tradition of private tutors and educational isolationism, she was not prepared to send Charles to the nearest local school. From her grandmother and her mother she had learned that majesty has its dignity, and she has never agreed with the 'bicycle-king' image of the Scandinavian monarchs. So it was likely that Charles would go to some sort of public school when he was thirteen. This being so, it then seemed best that he should go to a preparatory school where he could learn, as did other boys, to stand on his own feet from an early age, without the assurance of the nightly return to the security of his own home.

Prince Philip had been a pupil at Cheam School when it had been at the Surrey village of that name. By 1934 Cheam had become a densely populated suburb of expanding London, and the school was rebuilt at Headley on the Berkshire downs. Philip was convinced that his old school would provide an ideal preparatory educa- tion for his son. The Queen insisted on visiting many schools, ostensibly as part of the royal work, although each time she went to a boarding school the press assured the world that this was the one. She also invited several headmasters to the Palace, though she did not call in the joint headmasters of Prince Philip's old school. But in August 1957 it was decided that he should leave Hill House after a very pleasant two terms and, at the tender age of almost nine, leave home to become a pupil at the boarding school in Berkshire. During the holidays he visited the school along with his sister, father and mother. The Queen tested the beds in the dormitories as any thoughtful mother might. Her remark, 'Well, you won't be able to bounce on *these*

35

beds,' tells us a good deal about her awareness of her children's behaviour in their Palace nursery.

When the time came for Charles to go to Cheam, the family travelled overnight by rail from Balmoral to London. From here the Queen and Prince Philip drove him down to the school. For the first time in his life Charles was away from his Palace home, among strangers. Here he had to share a dormitory with seven other boys, and to get used to the unheated room with its uncarpeted floor and its ever-open windows. He had to make his own bed, clean his own shoes, fold his own clothes and altogether learn to do without the aid of a nurse, nanny or servants.

During the holidays the headmasters had written to the parents of the other ninety or so boys at the school:

> The purpose of this letter is to assure you that it is the wish of the Queen and Prince Philip that there shall be no alteration in the way the school is run, and that Charles shall be treated in exactly the same way as other boys. The staff will call him and refer to him as Prince Charles, but the boys will call him Charles. . . . His parents' wishes are that he should be given exactly the same education and upbringing as other boys in the school.

There were some ways in which it was relatively easy to treat him in the same way as other boys. He wore the same uniform of grey flannel suit and blue cap with a gold 'C' – for Cheam and not Charles. He followed the same timetable from the time a master shouted into the dormitory at 7.15 am, 'Rise and shine.' Like the others, he was inspected by the matron after he had washed and dressed, went to morning prayers in the school hall and, a Cheam tradition, shook hands with the headmasters. He took his turn in waiting on the other boys in the dining hall, where he sat on one of the long wooden benches around bare wooden tables. Lessons began at nine o'clock, with a morning break at about 10.30 for a glass of milk and a bun. Then there were more lessons before a one o'clock lunch. In the afternoons he and the other boys had a chance to do less academic things. On two afternoons they played games – rugby and soccer in the winter, cricket and swimming in the summer. On other afternoons the boys had art or handicraft, both of which the young Prince enjoyed. Tea was at six o'clock and by seven the boys were in bed, except on Saturday when the school provided a film show as a treat.

It was, in some senses, easy to treat the Prince as just another boy who had to slot into the well organized life of Cheam. But it was not as simple as that. On his first Sunday he was embarrassed by the sniggers of the other boys when the minister at the village church offered special prayers for the royal family, naming Prince Charles in

A happy first-day-of-term smile for Mr Peter Beck, headmaster of Charles' new school, Cheam, where he was a boarder. This was a difficult time for Charles, a shy nine-year-old who took some time to overcome the barriers created by his unique position.

When he was fourteen Charles went ski-ing in Switzerland. Here he takes a few tentative steps before making his descent.

particular. At Hill House the boys had been too young to be worried about abstracts such as class, colour or race. It was enough that a boy was 'a good chap', which in under-eight parlance had its own meaning. At Cheam the boys were older, and therefore aware that the new boy was rather special. Indeed, the letter from the head-masters and the ensuing talks with parents may have unintentionally only served to emphasize the special nature of their new companion. How was he to be treated? Anyone who went out of his way to make the new boy's first few days more pleasant may have been accused of 'sucking up'. The unfortunate, but probably inevitable, result was that for a while the already shy Prince was very much on his own.

It took some time for Charles to break down the barriers created by his own shyness and other boys' diffidence. His parents played their part in this. Each boy was allowed to have a model yacht which was raced on Sundays on the school pond. Charles sent home to ask if he might have one. When it arrived it was, very significantly, not the largest, tallest or glossiest, but among the smallest. Charles, like the other junior boys with whom he studied, ate, and shared a dormitory, had twenty-five shillings pocket money each term, and – like other boys – he was forced to resort to selling marbles and penknives when he ran short of money.

He himself played his own part in helping to break down the invisible barriers which separated him from the other boys. They were glad to discover that he was hopeless at mathematics – that made him seem more normal. They did not resent his ability in history or geography or his interest in painting, music and craft. Slowly, they accepted him as one of themselves, so that he enjoyed his time as a scout cub, and learned to defend himself from the school bully, who had succeeded in ducking him under a cold water tap in the school washroom, but who must have been surprised by the way the younger and smaller Charles ripped into him and pushed him into a bath full of water. Maybe one sign of acceptance was evident when, during a game of rugby, the plump Charles was one of the scrum which collapsed; a voice was heard yelling, 'Get off me, Fatty.'

During that very uncertain first term at Cheam the Prince, the school and the other pupils suffered because of the activities of press reporters and photographers who hung around the school and the village, trying to interview boys, servants, teachers, shop-keepers and anyone who might have a royal titbit to throw away. During the Christmas holidays Richard Colville, the Queen's press secretary, called editors of the national press to a meeting at Buckingham Palace where headmaster Peter Beck explained that the hordes of reporters hanging around Cheam School were beginning to have a detrimental effect on life at what had been a quiet school in the countryside. Colville explained that while the Queen and Prince Philip were anxious to break with royal tradition and have Charles educated with other boys, if the press continued to annoy him as they had done in the first term, the experiment would have to be called off. Fortunately the editors took the warning seriously; the hounds were called off and life at Cheam returned to something like normal, although most newspapers had a photograph of the Prince lining up with other boys to hand in his ticket at the railway station at Newbury, where he and the rest had to wait for the school bus to take them out to the school.

In his second term the Prince changed in a number of ways. He continued to grow, but, with all the football and swimming, lost some of his puppy fat. He also changed from the serious, shy boy who had gone to Cheam a few months earlier to a boy who, like the rest, laughed a good deal. He was also more confident in his relationships with other boys. During the summer term he had a present of a new cricket bat. When he first went to Cheam he had been afraid to offer the other boys any of the chocolates which his parents had given him as a parting gift. In the summer he was, like a normal boy, quite eager to let everyone have a go with the new bat.

Charles' first year at Cheam was to end in July 1958, but not without a very special surprise. The Empire and Commonwealth Games were held at Cardiff, the capital of Wales. Unfortunately the Queen was too ill to attend the Games herself. Having caught a serious chill after spending hours in the pouring rain during the Trooping of the Colour in June, she had gone on a long tour of Scotland and the North-East: she had to call off this tour after her cold worsened, and she had to have an operation to relieve catarrhal sinusitis. This meant that a longstanding plan for a visit to Wales which would have ended with her attendance at the closing ceremony of the Games, also had to be cancelled. Prince Philip was to attend as her deputy. However, the Queen had recorded a message which was to be played at the closing ceremonies. Charles had let a few of his close friends at Cheam into the secret. These 'lucky few' were allowed to listen to this closing ceremony in the headmaster's sitting-room. The almost nine-year-old Duke of Cornwall sat with his friends and listened to Prince Philip speak and then introduce the Queen's recording:

> By a cruel stroke of fate, I have been prevented from visiting north and south Wales and seeing something of the British and Commonwealth Games. I regret particularly not being with you in Cardiff today for the closing ceremonies of this great meeting of Commonwealth athletes. I am glad to say that I have been able to watch many of the competitions on television, and I was especially impressed by the atmosphere of good-natured sportsmanship which attended all the events. The Games would have been an undoubted success from every point of view and I would like to congratulate all the many people who have worked so hard to

39

perfect the arrangements. I want to take this opportunity of speaking to all Welsh people, not only in this arena, but wherever they may be. The British Empire and Commonwealth Games in the capital, together with all the activities of the Festival of Wales, have made a memorable year for the Principality. . . .

She paused, then went on quietly:

I have, therefore, decided to mark it further by an act which will, I hope, give as much pleasure to all Welshmen as it does to me. I intend to create my son, Charles, Prince of Wales today. When he is grown up I will present him to you at Caernarvon. . . .

The surprise was so complete that, for a moment, the crowd maintained that almost reverent quiet with which they had listened to the earlier part of the speech. Then the full implication of what had been said dawned on the 36,000 crowd, almost all of them Welsh, packed into the Cardiff stadium. They roared their welcome, and threw their programmes, hats, sunshades and dignity to the wind. They cheered Prince Philip as he circled the field in an open car and then sang as the band played a tune dedicated in a special way to the Prince of Wales:

Among our ancient mountains
And from our lovely vales,
Oh, let the pray'r re-echo,
'God bless the Prince of Wales!'

With heart and voice awaken
Those minstrel strains of yore,
Till Britain's name and glory
Resound from shore to shore.

As Prince of Wales, Charles was also Earl of Chester and was entitled to be a Knight of the Garter. But, just as the Queen intended that the publicity of the investiture should wait until he was grown up, so too his installation as a Knight of the Garter had to wait. Meanwhile, in the study at Cheam on that last Saturday of the term, the young Prince of Wales, glad to have heard his mother's voice, proud of the ancient title which he could now use, looked forward to going home on the following day.

When he returned to Cheam after the family holiday at Balmoral Charles was more at ease, particularly since there was a batch of new boys younger than him. Over the

Cheers! Charles raises his glass at the wedding of Lady Pamela Mountbatten to David Hicks.

next four years he grew in wisdom and experience. His school reports showed that he was 'above average in intelligence', well fitted to go on to some public school where he would take his 'o' and 'a' levels. His reports show that his main interests were in out-of-class activities, and in this he resembled his father. He learned to play the piano, sang in the church choir, regularly showed his art work at the school exhibition and enjoyed carpentry. Like his mother, he showed a natural talent on the stage – the result, perhaps, of years of playing charades at home. Charles played the Duke of Gloucester (Richard III) in one play in which he had to say 'and soon may I ascend the throne', which amused the audience if not the actor. During the perform-ance of this play on 19 February 1960 the headmaster came in to announce the birth of Prince Andrew.

Charles continued to play, if not to enjoy, school games, sometimes playing for the first cricket eleven and, in his last year, becoming captain of the first soccer eleven – in a season in which Cheam lost every game! He preferred individual sports, particularly swimming, and, although never as keen as Princess Anne, he became a proficient horseman. During his years at Cheam the Queen and Prince Philip visited him, as did other parents, about three times a term, while the Queen Mother also came on a couple of occasions. On these visits, the 'royals' came as parents, with no attendants and the minimum of fuss, although one stipulation was that no one was allowed to use a camera. While he was at Cheam Charles had the various childhood illnesses: he had chickenpox at Easter 1959, so that his Easter holiday was prolonged. He broke an ankle falling on the school stairs during the winter term – when he went home for Christmas he was still hobbling around in plaster, and earning a family nickname of 'Hopalong'. In February 1962 he was rushed to the Children's Hospital at Great Ormond Street where his appendix was removed. During his convalescence after this operation the thirteen-year-old Charles was allowed to take his absent father's place as host at one of the informal luncheons at the Palace. The growing Prince was being introduced into another section of royal life. He was also growing into a young man with a personality of his own – thoughtful, open-hearted, hard-working and willing to learn.

During holidays he followed the usual 'royal tour' around the four royal houses. While the family was at home at the Palace, Misspee took Prince Charles and Princess Anne to places of interest in London – Battersea Park, Westminster Abbey, Regent's Park Zoo and Scotland Yard, among others. His mother also arranged for him to have holiday tutors. At Easter 1959 Michael Fairbrother was brought in again; during the summer of 1959 a French-Canadian stayed at Balmoral to help with Prince Charles' French. Charles spent a good deal of his holidays with his father, who took him out as a member of shooting parties at Sandringham, taught him to drive a car when he was eleven, and also showed him the rudiments of polo at which, in time, he became very proficient. While he never equalled his father's enthusiasm for sailing, he excelled him at fishing, a hobby which he shares with his mother and grandmother.

Maybe more significantly, his father taught him how to get on with people, how to work hard and to get to the heart of whatever it is that he is about. The growing self-confidence of the young Prince as he entered his early teens owed a great deal to Prince Philip, to the men who had taught him at Hill House and Cheam, to his mother's care in the choice of nurses and nannies as well as teachers, but above all to his own ability to absorb the lessons and examples that were offered him.

The young Prince was a guest at the wedding of his aunt Margaret to Antony Armstrong-Jones in May 1960, and at the wedding of the Duke of Kent and Miss Katharine Worsley at York Minster in September 1961. After that wedding he went back for his last year at Cheam, aware that the royal weddings had sparked off once again the press interest in 'the woman he will marry'. The list of favourites was as long as the list of reporters and, indeed, of schools which, the papers assured us, 'he will attend next year'.

The Queen introduced him gradually into public life; he was allowed to read the lessons at Sandringham church, but not to open the new Tamar Bridge which linked his duchy with Plymouth and Devon. During the Easter holidays in 1962 he went with his father on a semi-private visit to some of his German relatives. Now that Britain is a member of the EEC, and visits to and from German politicians are commonplace, it is difficult to accept that in 1962 there had still been no official visit by a member of the royal family to Germany, where the British Army of the Rhine was a symbol of both World War II and of the two countries' joint membership of NATO. Prince Charles' visit helped the reconciliation between the two countries which was already under way, and was so necessary if Britain was to become a fully integrated member of the EEC.

4
At Gordonstoun
and Timbertop
1961-7

In November 1961 Prince Charles had his thirteenth birthday and serious consideration had to be given to the question of the school he would attend after Cheam. Some
thought he might go to Eton. But Eton was too near London and the British press
would have found it all too easy to keep close watch on the growing Prince. The
Queen relied on her husband's advice. He, after all, had been to school in Britain,
whereas the Queen had no direct experience of the many and varied boys' schools.

Prince Philip seems to have taken into consideration both the needs of the
monarchy as an institution and of his son as an individual. Charles' own bent – in
interests and studies – was, and still is, towards the past. Already a keen historian, he
was later to become an enthusiastic archaeologist. There was no danger that he would
fail to appreciate, as monarch, that he formed part of a historic tradition. But Prince
Philip believes that the royal family must also be concerned with the future, with the
way in which the country, its industry and institutions are developing. This makes it
essential for the monarch to be forward-looking as well as tradition-minded. Charles
had already lost much of that shyness and reserve which had made his first term at
Cheam a period of unhappiness. But he was still not as self-reliant and confident as
his extrovert father would have liked him to be, and as Charles himself might wish
to be when called on to play an active role as heir and later as monarch. Prince
Philip's views on education are summed up in part of one of his own speeches:
'There can be no doubt that all schools have a threefold responsibility of training the
intellect, actively developing the character, and providing a practical preparation for
life. . . . After all, it is the qualities of initiative and perseverance, qualities of the spirit,
which are going to make the best use of the trained intellect.' There is little doubt that,
when making that speech, Prince Philip had in mind the training he had received at
his old school at Gordonstoun in Scotland.

Gordonstoun has its origins in Salem, the school which had been founded in 1919 by Prince Max of Baden, the last Chancellor of Imperial Germany which had been defeated in World War I and, after the abdication of the Kaiser, replaced by the Weimar Republic. Prince Max was anxious that the defeat of Germany should not lead to a continuation of that bitterness, that sense of failure and hopelessness which was evident in post-war Germany. In his castle at Salem he founded a school and his first pupils were the sons of the German nobility whom he hoped to train for the leadership of a new Germany. He hoped to replace the traditional landowning *junkers* of Prussia with a new elite which would be less rigid and more humanitarian, less conscious of rights and privileges and more aware of duties and service. Kurt Hahn was appointed as headmaster.

In 1929 Prince Max died, and in 1933 Hahn was forced to flee from Nazi Germany because he was a Jew and because he had criticized the brutal methods used by the Nazis. Hahn opened a new school on the Gordonstoun estate near Elgin in Scotland. Here, in a seventeenth-century house standing in 300 acres of land, the school started in the summer term of 1934 with three boys and a small number of teachers.

Hahn had been a Rhodes Scholar at Oxford before World War I and had learned to admire the British public school system which, he declared, enabled a man to be 'taught to argue without quarrelling, to quarrel without suspecting and to suspect without slandering'. At Salem, and later at Gordonstoun, he did his best to take what was advantageous from that older system and to avoid the dangers arising from the highly academic and almost monastic life of those schools. While paying attention to academic attainment, the school would do much more. Boys would be taught the value of service to others in the community nearby and further afield. They would also be helped to develop stamina through physical labour and manly pursuits – hence the curriculum of rescue training, sailing, forestry, mountaineering, athletics and expeditions, which were also intended to develop initiative.

It is ironic that, in Germany, Hahn was accused of trying to undermine Prussian manhood by his policy of anglicization, while in Britain he was accused of introducing Prussian ideals into the British system. In both countries his methods were condemned as being too spartan. In this the critics showed that they knew little about the original Spartan system which had been intended to make or break a body; only the fittest survived to become the city-state's ruling elite. In Gordonstoun no boy was made or broken; he was helped to develop self-control and self-reliance, and to realize his own full potential. Indeed, if there is a Greek origin to Hahn's ideas it is to be found in Athens, not Sparta, in the *Republic* of Plato rather than in the heroics of Thermopylae.

The Queen appreciated that Prince Philip owed a great deal to his old school, but she was not certain that the Gordonstoun regime would necessarily suit her introverted son. In October 1961 she visited the school and was pleasantly surprised to find that it was much less austere than some of its critics had led her to believe. On 23 January 1962 an announcement came from the Palace that the Prince of Wales would commence his studies at Gordonstoun on 1 May, the beginning of the summer term. One newspaper spoke of the 'rigours of exercise in the northern twilight'. The *Daily Mail* commented: 'The rather more rigorous disciplines of a school which is in some ways less conventional than others will do the young prince no harm. Besides which he will find more freedom and less public distraction in Scotland than he ever would nearer London. If he gets on as well at Gordonstoun as he has at Cheam he'll do all right. Good luck to him, and may his school days be happy.'

Charles finished his last term at Cheam – appendix operation and all. During the Easter holidays he had the pleasure of welcoming his father home from a tour of Latin America, and on 1 May the old boy flew the new boy to Gordonstoun in his own Heron. Prince Philip pointed out the room where he used to live when he was at the school, and introduced Charles to the headmaster, Mr Chew, who had been Prince Philip's housemaster. The head boy or guardian joined the party which showed Charles around the school's main block in the castle-like building. They then went about a quarter of a mile to Windmill Lodge, the low stone and timber building which was to be Charles' home and his school 'house' for the next few years. Here he met the housemaster, Mr Whitby, and the head of the house. Prince Philip had lunch at the school, and then drove off to Lossiemouth and his aircraft. He piloted the plane over his old school and waggled his wings as a final salute to Gordonstoun and its newest pupil.

During his first term Prince Charles suffered once more from loneliness and from the attentions of the press. An appeal was issued from the Palace towards the end of April 1962:

> When publicity was reduced at the end of the first term at Cheam School, it became possible for the whole school to function in the normal way and therefore the Prince of Wales was able to receive a normal education. . . . For this the Queen and the Duke of Edinburgh are grateful, and I am asked to say that they hope that this happy state of affairs may continue during the Prince of Wales's stay at Gordonstoun. Her Majesty and His Royal Highness fully understand the very natural interest in the Prince of Wales's education, but they feel that he will only be able to derive full benefit from his days at school if he is not made the centre of special attention.

This, it was hoped, would take care of one of the problems that had affected the early days at Cheam. But there was nothing that could help the still reserved thirteen-year-old who found himself a new boy again, one of the young ones, and a member of what must have seemed a strange organization with its uniform of shirt and shorts, its emphasis on trust rather than imposed discipline, and its constant theme of achievement, service, physical fitness and activity. Once again he felt the positive disadvantage of being Prince of Wales, known as Charles to the boys and Prince Charles to the staff, each of whom would have to be called 'Sir'. A former pupil recalled Prince Philip's time at the school: 'The school has never respected titles much. The Prince of Wales's father was expected to live down, not to enjoy, the privileges of his birth. Had he, for one moment, sought to impose such notions on those who were struggling with him to parse Ovid, he would not have been allowed to forget his presumption for many a term.'

The hut which served as a dormitory for Charles and fifty-nine others was bleaker than anything he had yet known – bare wooden floors, unpainted walls, no furniture except for the beds, and three naked electric light bulbs hanging from the ceiling. While senior boys had the luxury of a rubber mattress, Charles and other juniors had to be content with horsehair mattresses on iron-framed beds. Clothes were kept in a locker room. In the dining-rooms at the main house the boys sat fourteen to a table, and Charles took his turn to serve the others. Lessons were taken in the main block, or in one of the huts nearby, where there was also accommodation for private study during free time, of which there was little enough.

The day began with one of the boys, the 'waker', getting the others up at 6.45 am. In a uniform of blue jersey and shorts the boys went on what is described as 'an easy run around the garden' followed by a warm bath and a cold shower – the first of the day's two compulsory cold showers. Then the boys had to clean their shoes, make beds, and sweep their share of the dormitory and its corridors before going to the main house for breakfast at 8.15. Morning prayers lasted for ten minutes from 8.55. The rest of the morning was divided into five lessons, each of forty minutes. On most mornings one of these was designated a 'training break' when, under the supervision of the physical training master, the boys would run, jump, throw the discus and javelin as well as tackle an assault course.

Lunch was at 1.20 pm, followed by a period of twenty minutes during which the boys lay on the floor while a master read aloud or music was played. The afternoons consisted of various outdoor activities. On three afternoons a week there were organized games, seamanship or practical work on the estate which had to be maintained by the boys. Logs had to be chopped, fences repaired and, Prince Charles' task for most of the first term, dustbins had to be emptied. While the boys were given freedom

47

of choice on some afternoons, they had to spend one afternoon on one or other of the estate services; some boys helped out the local coastguards, some trained as sea cadets, others did scouting, helped the fire service or trained as members of the school's mountain and surf rescue teams. During his time at the school Prince Charles tried his hand at all these. On one afternoon the boys were free to work at their own individual projects which were exhibited at the end of each year. Saturday afternoon was devoted to matches or expeditions. At four o'clock every afternoon – except the free afternoon – the Prince and the rest of the pupils had their second warm bath and cold shower before taking tea, which was followed by two more periods of lessons. Supper was eaten at 6.20, followed by homework or a meeting of some school society. At 9.15 came bedtime and a period of five minutes of complete silence for meditation and relaxation. Then, after a ten-minute interval, lights were out at 9.30 pm.

Charles had captained a soccer eleven at Cheam. At Gordonstoun the school game was rugby and, although the Prince of Wales was chosen to play for the junior colts in one home game, his interest soon waned and he preferred to spend his time with some of the people he met around the estate and in the neighbourhood. In this way he got to know a large number of people of all ages and classes.

The Queen Mother drove over from Birkhall, her home on the Balmoral estate, to visit her grandson at weekends and to take him back with her for a few hours. No doubt she congratulated him when he got his life-saving certificate and succeeded in negotiating the commando course. Maybe she commiserated with him when he complained – about being away from the rest of the family, or about the non-stop pattern of the day. It is probable that she shared his parents' pleasure when, in July of his first term, they visited the school and saw Charles' contribution to the school exhibition of arts and crafts. Charles had already shown that he enjoyed carpentry; at Gordonstoun he learned pottery and produced a number of pots, jugs, mugs and ornamental pieces. Before he left the school for his first summer holiday he had learned how to capsize his canoe and right it again, and had made such all-round progress that he would be qualified to change, in the evenings of the following term, into a special uniform which was Gordonstoun's mark of his ascent to the first rung of promotion. His school report said that he was academically 'well up . . . very near the top of his class'. All in all, the experiment had begun well.

During the summer holidays of 1962 Charles sailed through the Scottish lochs and canals in the new royal racing yawl, the sixty-three-foot *Bloodhound*, along with his sister, Anne, and his German cousin, Guelf. During this holiday at Balmoral, he and his parents decided that, in the coming year, as a member of the upper fourth, he would take his favourite languages – French and German – English, history, geog-

Arriving at London Airport having flown from Gordonstoun to spend a weekend with his family at Windsor. The press inevitably commented on the Prince's 'Beatle' hair-do, but officials were quick to reply that Charles' hair was merely windswept.

raphy and whichever of the sciences interested him most. As a capable seaman he was already interested in and adept at navigation, which gave him some interest in applied science. This course of study was intended to provide him with sufficient grasp of the sciences that, given his inquisitive mind, he would, in the future, be able to ask the right questions whenever he was involved in discussions on scientific and technical issues.

On his return to Gordonstoun in the autumn, the Prince of Wales was proud to wear the evening uniform of grey-blue trousers and a light blue sweater. However, the other boys insisted on initiating him into the privileged ranks of wearers of School Uniform with capital letters. As he was changing on the first evening a gang of boys seized him in the locker room of Windmill Lodge, ran him along to the shower room and heaved him into a bath full of cold water. This was his schoolfellows' way of accepting him as another ordinary boy who had started to make his mark in the closed society of the school.

During the Christmas holidays he had another initiation, this time arranged by the Queen and Prince Philip. In January 1963 he went on his own to Bavaria to visit his uncle, Prince George, with whose family he was to have his first ski-ing holiday at the Swiss mountain resort of Tarasp. Crowds of reporters, photographers and sensation seekers poured into the tiny village whose population was doubled by the influx of Charles-watchers. In *The Weekly Tribune* of Geneva, McIver Campbell wrote:

> *The greatest show on snow has just ended and the players have struck camp, once again to follow the young man from whom, in Switzerland, they stole the lime-light. Yet, while here, they provided plenty of entertainment. To the amusement of all . . . or nearly all.*
>
> *Yet even Prince Ludwig of Hesse admitted to me, none too enthusiastically, 'It's comic opera, there's no other word for it, it really is.' He was of course, describing the antics of the European Press in covering the first visit to Switzer-land of Prince Charles, heir to the British throne, skiing's latest devotee. . . . It was, practically speaking, the first time that Prince Charles was confronted with the press* en masse, *almost on his own. His father would have been proud of him. . . .*

Charles posed for the photographers and then asked them: 'Haven't you got enough pictures now?' His aunt, Princess Margarete of Hesse, asked the crowd of sightseers, 'Please leave us alone. He only has eight days to learn to ski and to have some fun at it.' But no one paid any attention. Indeed, as Campbell relates, the Prince had to learn, as had his father, to handle the press in his own way:

The funeral of Sir Winston Churchill. Members of the Royal Family wait on the steps of St Paul's while the coffin is placed on the gun-carriage after the service.

Shortly afterwards, a royal command almost boomed across the snow-covered hills. As a photographer attempted to slip unnoticed up the path, towards Schloss Tarasp, in close proximity to the royal residence, Prince Charles poked his head out of an upstairs window and (pardon me) bawled: 'Hey! Where are you going?' The startled photographer, crestfallen, was led downhill by the omnipresent Superintendent Frank Kelly, Prince Philip's personal bodyguard, who had been detailed for the Swiss visit.

The pressmen chased after Charles and his companions across snow slopes for which they were ill-clad and ill-shod, falling into drifts and getting cold and wet – all in the name of the freedom to plague the royals. For the next few days Charles took his ski-ing lessons in the grounds of the Hesse *schloss*. But on the Sunday, press and Prince had another confrontation, as Campbell recorded:

However, at the weekend, the photographers had another chance to focus on their target. As the Prince set off on a two-hour sleigh ride on Sunday, they waited at the first corner with their shutters cocked. The Prince was forewarned, and fore-armed with his own camera, a 35mm model similar to many in the battery of apparatus aimed at him. He calmly and repeatedly clicked the shutter, tongue-in-cheek. With a concerted howl of disappointment, mixed with laughter, the cameramen took to the road in pursuit, in a long convoy of cars bearing half a dozen different national number-plates. It was like a snow scene from a Keystone Kops movie as impatient voices bawled suggestions in English, French, Italian, and German, the cars revving madly, wheels spinning, as they leaped, slithered and bumped into each other in a frantic race for the best positions behind the speeding sleighs.

In spite of the attentions which spoilt the holiday and blighted the Queen's hope that he might have a pleasantly ordinary time, Charles received twenty-five marks out of a possible twenty-eight in his first ski-ing test and won a gold medal – almost a modern equivalent of the spurs granted to a former Prince of Wales, the Black Prince.

During his third term at Gordonstoun the Queen instructed the Kings of Arms to register her son's coat-of-arms or armorial 'achievement'. These consist of a shield divided into four quarters, two representing England, while Wales and Scotland have a quarter each. The shield, supported by an English lion and a Scottish unicorn, is surmounted by the crest of a crowned lion and encircled with the blue banner and the Prince of Wales' own motto, '*Ich Dien*' (I serve). In the middle of the great shield is a smaller one, surmounted by the Prince's coronet and divided into four quarters, coloured red and gold, with the four leopards signifying Llewellyn the Great and the other native princes of Wales. Under the shield, and between the Prince of Wales' three feathers and the Welsh dragon, appear the fifteen gold pieces which denote his duchy of Cornwall. It is this coat-of-arms which appears on the Prince's banner above his stall in the Garter Chapel of St George at Windsor. This was a public mark of the Prince's growing maturity. To the fourteen-year-old Charles in the summer term at Gordonstoun, perhaps a more immediate mark of approval came when he was enrolled in the junior training plan, Gordonstoun's second step along the promotion road.

During this term he qualified to become one of the crew which sailed the school ketch, the *Pinta*, around the Outer Hebrides – one of Gordonstoun's traditional maritime exercises designed to foster a sense of comradeship, achievement and inde-pendence through hard work in difficult conditions. The *Pinta*, a rigged yacht with a great spread of canvas, was a centre of attraction whenever she put into anchorage. On Monday 17 June the ship arrived at Stornoway on the Isle of Lewis. Charles and the rest of the crew were given leave to have lunch at a local hotel and to go to the cinema. His private detective went off to get the tickets while the boys waited in the hotel lounge. Here they became the centre of a peep-show, since the locals had recog-nized the *Pinta* and had found out that the Prince was ashore. To escape from the crowd peering in through the lounge window, Charles went into another room which turned out to be the bar. Here, the fourteen-year-old ordered a cherry brandy, which he was given whenever he went shooting at Sandringham. He might have got away with this contravention of the law if it had not been for a freelance journalist who came into the bar. She made sure that the story was splashed around the world. The private detective at first denied that the incident had occurred. However, the Palace later issued a statement apologizing for the denial, which only enabled the press to continue to run the story. The *Daily Mail*, acting as defender of the royals while still managing to get mileage out of the 'scandal', declared:

> *Let there be no hypocritical holding up of hands in horror over the affair of the Prince of Wales and the cherry brandy. He went into a bar, bought the drink, and downed it. It was wrong of him, but in a school which believes fervently in free-dom, such things are bound to happen among boys of spirit. What more could be expected? The Prince of Wales is fourteen. He may have been led into this prank, but he will pay for it in punishment from the headmaster. If no action against the innkeeper is taken it will not be because a royal boy was concerned. Court proceedings do not usually follow the accidental serving of alcohol to per-sons under age. It is only when the offence is several times repeated that a charge*

is laid. Lastly, a word of congratulations to the Palace for its courage and frank-
ness in stating that it had been wrong to deny a story correctly given by the Press.

Most people supported the lenient view expressed by the *Dail Mail*'s cartoonist, who showed one Scot saying to another: 'I wouldna ha' minded if he'd had a wee drap o' Scotch.' Charles was reprimanded by his headmaster, temporarily lost his place in the junior training plan, and had learned the hard lesson that a royal error will be magnified by a sensation-mongering press. It is hardly surprising that he now shares his father's jaundiced views on the press and press photographers.

However, life at Gordonstoun had to go on in spite of the incident of the cherry brandy. Charles worked hard and won back his place on the training plan. He also joined the Combined Cadet Force, spending the first two years in the army section where, like the rest, he had his share of square-bashing, route marching and field days. He also learned map reading, field cookery and first aid. Later on he joined the naval section of the Cadet Force, spending some time at the Portsmouth training camp, HMS *Vernon*. Here he was shouted at by petty officers, had lessons in diving, learned about torpedoes, anti-submarine tactics and minesweeping. His liking for the sea was confirmed by his period at *Vernon* which he enjoyed more than he did his period in the army section of the Force.

He had always shown an interest in music. In 1964 he played the trumpet in the school orchestra at a concert given in St Giles' Cathedral on St David's Day, and was a member of the choir which sang at that concert. While he enjoyed the trumpet, and played jazz and pop as well as classical music, he was later to turn to the cello, perhaps a more fitting instrument for his position. His interest in history was given an added dimension when he took part in an archaeological dig in a cave at Covesea near Gordonstoun. This new activity encouraged wider reading and laid foundations for a more mature interest in this subject which he showed while in Australia and as an undergraduate.

During this year Charles was allowed to go to London to see his new brother Edward, born on 10 March 1964, the third of the Queen's sons to be born in a leap year. While at the Palace he had a chance to see Misspee, now busy training the ebullient Prince Andrew who envied Charles' freedom to go to school outside the Palace gates. But Prince Charles knew that life at school was not all honey, as the confined Andrew may have thought. For example, he had to face the onset of 'o' levels, to be taken in the summer of 1964. Prince Charles was the first heir to the throne to sit a public examination, to have his abilities tested and the results publi-cized by the press. The results were relatively good: he obtained passes in Latin,

French, history and English language and literature. However, he failed in physics and mathematics, and had to re/take these in December 1965, when he was successful in spite of his inherent dislike of mathematics and his inherited slowness in the subject.

At the end of the summer holidays, which had been spent as usual at Balmoral, Charles, together with his sister and father, went to Athens to represent the British royal family at the wedding of King Constantine of Greece to the Danish Princess Anne/Marie, once a press favourite to marry Charles himself. Prince Philip was related to both the bride and the bridegroom; Princess Anne was one of five brides/maids and Charles was one of the ten young men who took turns to hold the golden crown over the bridegroom's head, part of the service in the Greek Orthodox Church. It was, in fact, a family affair.

The few days after the wedding became a pleasant holiday during which Prince Charles and Princess Anne, together with some of the younger members of the Swedish royal family and the German cousins, used the facilities of the Astir beach club about twelve miles from Athens. Greek naval police patrolled in paddle boats to keep the press and other sightseers away. However some French photographers, in their own paddle boat, slipped through the cordon of patrol boats and made their way towards the raft on which Charles and some of the others were sunbathing. The click of the cameras acted like a Pavlovian signal. Charles and some of the other boys slipped off the raft, took hold of the paddle boat and succeeded in rocking it so violently that two of the photographers were tipped into the sea, while the third, seeking to hold his balance, lost his camera overboard. Unfortunately for the publicity/shy Charles, the camera was retrieved, the films developed and the pictures of sunbathing royals became front/page news all round the world.

This clash between the Prince and the press served as a preliminary to what became a nine/days' wonder as 'the affair of the olive green exercise book'. One of the dozens of exercise books which the Prince had used in his two years at Gordonstoun was stolen from his room. It was stamped with his name and contained some of his weekly essays. The headmaster warned the police that this 'collector's piece' had been stolen; it was soon discovered that the book was being offered for sale to newspapers and press agencies under the lurid and misleading title of 'The Confessions of Prince Charles'. The essays made interesting reading for voyeurs anxious to know what the Prince thought about such topics as 'The press, wireless and television services' and 'What four things I would take with me in the event of a nuclear emergency and evacuation to a place of safety'. Charles' objection to the public appearance of his essays was not that he was ashamed of them, for indeed they drew favourable com/ment for what that was worth – he deplored the fact that the book had been stolen.

As the Palace commented: 'It is highly regrettable that the private essays of a school-boy should have been published in this way.' The American magazine *Time* quoted other newspaper reports that 'the princely pauper' had sold his essay book to get extra pocket money. On this the Queen's press secretary, Richard Colville, wrote:

> *In the first place he is too intelligent and old enough to realize how embarrassing this would turn out to be, and second, he is only too conscious of the interest of the Press in anything to do with himself and his family. The suggestion that his parents keep him so short of money that he has to find other means to raise it is also a complete invention. . . . The police would not have attempted to regain the composition book unless they were satisfied that it had been obtained illegally.*

Eventually Scotland Yard detectives found the book in Lancashire. In November, six weeks after it had first been reported as missing, the Mercury Press of St Helens issued a writ against the Metropolitan Police claiming that the goods had been wrongly taken from their possession. In fact, this was a bluff, but it rekindled interest in the story, and the press were given another opportunity to indulge in baiting the royals – the story rumbled on until well into the New Year and the start of a new term.

In January 1965 Sir Winston Churchill died, and Charles had leave from school to attend the funeral of the former Prime Minister with whom he had stood at West-minster pier to meet his mother on her return from her first Commonwealth tour nearly ten years before. The funeral was one of Charles' rare public appearances, but in itself was a sign that he was now to play a more prominent role. In April 1965, as another indication that he was growing up, he was allowed to attend a meeting of the eight-man council that administers the duchy of Cornwall.

At school Charles was promoted to the senior training plan, played games, went on expeditions, tackled his assigned projects and continued to develop his skill in craftwork and music. He was confirmed by the Archbishop of Canterbury during the Easter holiday, which was spent at Windsor and was enlivened by games of polo.

On 30 June 1965 he undertook what might be described as his first official public engagement. The Queen had invited 600 young people representing Scottish students, sports and youth organizations to a garden party at the Palace of Holyrood, her official residence in Scotland. Charles, now nearly seventeen, stood with his parents during the thirty-five-minute long reception of the guests. He showed that he had absorbed a great deal during his schooling, being able to talk to a wide variety of young people, to ask each a pertinent question or two so that he fully deserved the praise of *The New York Times* with its headlines: 'Prince Charles a Social Success: He's just a chip off the old Block; Britain's Royal Heir shows father's charming ways

A big ordeal for Charles – his first public engagement, a garden party which the Queen held for Scottish and Commonwealth students. He chatted naturally to the guests, and confided to one that he had failed two of his exams.

Receiving expert advice from his father during a polo game at Windsor. The day before Charles had played his first competitive game and scored two goals.

in meeting the public: Prince of Wales life of the party; takes after Dad. . . .' over a report which read:

> *At the end of the afternoon, Charles did what his father has done many times – got so interested in his conversation he was left behind when the royal party moved on. All the members of the Royal Household followed the Queen and Philip as they strolled back to the Palace, except Charles. He was still talking three minutes after his parents had left. Then an official of the Lord Chamberlain's office caught his eye and he quickly chased after his parents, reaching the palace just in time for the national anthem which ended the party.*

During his last year at the school Charles scored a great success as the lead in the school production of *Macbeth*, a play in which his father had played the small part of Donalbain when he was at Gordonstoun. The royal family has its own tradition of producing and playing in amateur theatricals. The Queen had enjoyed her own parts in Windsor Castle pantomimes and hoped that her son would lose some of his diffidence if he could learn to enjoy acting in front of an audience. His success in the part was all the greater because he played it in front of his parents who had flown up from London. He had other successes, too, during this term; he became a prefect, finally succeeded in passing mathematics at 'o' level, and gained his Duke of Edinburgh's award. All in all it was a good note on which to leave Gordonstoun.

From the day that he went to Cheam School, until he was seventeen in November 1965, the growing Prince had been 'following in father's footsteps'. He had made every effort to live up to the ideal embodied in his extrovert, sport-loving father. But in spite of his schooling and his own efforts, he remained at seventeen very different from his father. Charles was introspective and was not technologically minded; his chosen science was biology and his main interests continued to be history and archaeology – the past rather than the future.

Both parents and son decided that it was time that Charles escaped from his father's shadow, became more his own man, and had a different educational experience. Once again it was Prince Philip who pointed the way. He had stayed in Australia as a serving naval officer and, with the Queen, had enjoyed his time there during the Commonwealth tour. The Queen, during her last Australian tour, had promised that she would 'send my eldest son to visit you, too, when he is older'. This had been taken to mean that, at some later stage, the Prince of Wales would be sent on a series of overseas tours much as his great-uncle, the future Duke of Windsor, had undertaken in the 1920s and 1930s. But the Queen had more than that in mind, although there seems little doubt that the idea of the Prince attending an Australian school

Playing with fire-fighting equipment at Timbertop, where Charles got a taste of life in the Australian bush. His daily routine included cleaning out pig-sties, gardening and waiting at table.

came from his father. By chance, the Australian elder statesman, Sir Robert Menzies – a former Prime Minister and one of Churchill's great friends – was on holiday in Scotland in the autumn of 1965, and was invited to stay with the royal family at Balmoral. When asked about Australian schools in general, and in his own native state of Victoria in particular, he recommended the Church of England grammar school at Geelong in Victoria. On 19 November it was announced that the Prince of Wales would spend a term at Geelong, while a Geelong boy would take his place at Gordonstoun.

A Labour member of the Australian Parliament challenged the choice of school and asked why, if the Prince was to attend an Australian school, he was not going to one less exclusive than Geelong. Menzies replied:

> *I went to Balmoral at the request of the Queen and the Duke of Edinburgh, and had a talk with them. I was asked my advice. . . . I was quite detached, personally, because I went to another school which presumably, from the honourable member's question, isn't so exclusive or 'tony'. . . . I should be very sorry for the young prince if he were at school in the middle of a crowded city in Australia, with people gazing at him, with people trying to get pictures of him, and with people making him a raree-show. This isn't what he will be here for. He will be here to go to school and mix with ordinary Australian boys.*

In fact the Prince was not to attend the main school but its 'colony', about 200 miles away to the north. Here, about 2000 feet above sea level in wild, rough country on the lower slopes of Mount Timbertop, there was a Gordonstoun-type extension of the main school. It had been founded by a former headmaster who wanted to give the city-dwelling boys some idea of life in the bush. About 135 boys go from Geelong to Timbertop at any one time. They live in timber-built chalets, wear old clothes and follow an outdoor curriculum in addition to their normal studies. Trees have to be chopped for firewood and for fence-making, chickens and pigs are raised to provide food; gardening, fishing and climbing are other obligatory parts of the school day. One newspaper wondered if the Prince were 'genuinely enjoying a more contemporary education than Queen Victoria's heir, later King Edward VII. A modern education is no longer built on the theory that "toughness" moulds the character. Psychology has changed our views. Besides, the cold bath, the iron bedstead and the rigours of the lumber camp are not very relevant to the modern world.'

But the Queen had been to Geelong during her 1954 tour and had liked what she had seen. Most Australians welcomed the decision to send the heir to the throne to one of their schools. As Menzies said, it was:

> . . . a very tangible demonstration of the close ties between Australia and the royal family. The idea of the young Prince of Wales living and studying here in his formative years is a prospect that will give widespread satisfaction. It is an imaginative and practical step. Getting to know Australia through young Australians should prove of inestimable value for a prince whose future duties will require a comprehensive knowledge of the countries and peoples of the Commonwealth.

An Australian newspaper noted:

> Anglo-Australian relations are a curious business. The English regard the Australians as people who talk funny, and are generally crude, while the Australians call the English 'pommies' – which means a combination of sissy, snobbish and remote. Englishmen, in Australia, are looked upon as foreigners. . . . Prince Charles's fellow-students – mostly the sons of very rich Australian families – will presumably adopt an attitude based on the Aussie's instinctive anti-English egalitarianism. Australians tend, like Americans, to be violently extroverted, amiable and sensitive about snobbery. Since Prince Charles is a pleasant if somewhat shy young man and decidedly not given to snobbishness, he should get along well.

At the end of January the Prince left London Airport. Once again, as in the early days at Cheam and Gordonstoun, he was on his own, in a new situation, facing another crowd of strangers who might make life difficult for him. However, the crowd waiting at Sydney Airport gave him a warm welcome and the very informality of the 'Good on you, Charlie,' may have served to relieve his tensions. He had a pleasant couple of days relaxing in Canberra, sailing on Lake Burley Griffin, riding over the gentle hills of a nearby sheep station and looking over the local wildlife reserve at Gungahlin.

Then, on 3 February, he was driven to Timbertop. Here he was plunged into the life of the school; along with the others he chopped wood, cleaned dormitories and living quarters, gardened, cleaned out pig-sties and waited at table. He was quickly and genuinely accepted by the boys, who appreciated his ability at athletics and pottery and his initiative, which had earned him the silver medal of the Duke of Edinburgh's award scheme. He was a little older than most of the other boys, and they soon acknowledged him as a resourceful leader. He played lead trumpet in the band, went on an expedition to Papua and visited the Great Barrier Reef. In April his grandmother, who was touring Australia, visited him at Timbertop and remarked how he had grown and how well he looked.

The original idea had been that Charles was to spend only one term in Australia but that, if he liked it, he could stay for a second. He did stay, and enjoyed the second term even more than the first. However, in July the term came to an end and Charles had to fly home. He wrote a message for his equerry to read to the crowd gathered to see him off at Sydney Airport:

It would be difficult to leave without saying how much I have enjoyed and appreciated my stay in Australia and how touched I have been by the kindness of so many people in making these six months such a worthwhile experience. The most wonderful part was the opportunity to travel and see, at least, some of the country (I hope I shall be able to come back and see the rest) and also the chance to meet so many people which completes the link with a country I am very sad to be leaving; and yet I shall now be able to visualize Australia in the most vivid terms, after such a marvellous visit.

There was equal warmth in the statement of the headmaster:

Leaving aside the question of royalty, we have really enjoyed having Prince Charles at the School. Before his visit most Australians had very hazy and possibly erroneous ideas of him, if they had any ideas at all. They probably thought of him as just a distant, uninteresting figurehead. In future most of them will know him as a friendly, intelligent, natural boy with a good sense of humour, someone who by no means has an easy task ahead of him in life.

From Sydney Charles was flown to Jamaica to join Prince Philip and Princess Anne at the Commonwealth Games, where he was impressed by the friendliness of the people and the colour of the island, and was reminded that he had become Prince of Wales during similar games eight years previously. Then he returned to Gordonstoun, where he became head of Windmill Lodge, his father's old house, and completed his studies for 'A' levels. In July 1967 he sat his examinations in history and French. His results came through in September – he had passed in both subjects and got a distinction in his history optional paper, something achieved by only about six per cent of the 4000 or so candidates taking history for the Oxford and Cambridge schools examination board. Another milestone had been passed by a maturing Prince who had benefited from his time in Australia, was more at home at Gordonstoun than he had been during his first years there, and seemed fully prepared to go on to the next stage of his education.

5
The Undergraduate Prince
1967-70

In 1936 the new King, George VI, came to the throne with a ten-year-old Princess Elizabeth as the heir-apparent, a title signifying that the birth of a Prince to the King and Queen would make her second in line of succession. She was therefore only a 'temporary heir', as it were. In 1937 Parliament passed a Regency Act to provide for the governing of the country in the event of the King's death, which would leave an under-age princess as the sovereign. This Act declared that in the event of the King's death before Princess Elizabeth came of age at eighteen, the regent should be 'the person, twenty-one years or older, who was next in succession to the throne'. In 1937 the potential regent was named as the Queen's uncle, the Duke of Gloucester.

When Princess Margaret reached the age of twenty-one she took over the role of potential regent in the event that Princess Elizabeth died, leaving as heir to the throne the infant Charles. But in 1953, a few weeks before the coronation, Princess Margaret told her mother and sister that she wished to marry Group-Captain Peter Townsend, a former RAF pilot and, after 1944, an equerry and close friend to George VI. Under the Royal Marriages Act of 1772 members of the royal family in line of succession to the throne have to obtain the sovereign's consent if they wish to marry before reaching the age of twenty-five. Over that age, they still have to ask permission, but the sovereign's veto can only suspend any decision; after a year's delay the prince or princess involved is free to marry.

The problem about a marriage between Townsend and Princess Margaret was that in December 1952 he had obtained a divorce on the grounds of his wife's adultery. Even though he was the innocent party, marriage to a royal princess, and one who was the potential regent, would be an unfortunate beginning to the new reign. It would revive the controversy that had split the royal family and the nation in 1936 when Edward VIII had wanted to marry the twice-divorced Mrs Simpson. Prime Minister Winston Churchill advised the Queen that she ought to refuse permission for such a marriage, leaving Princess Margaret free to wait, if she so wished, until she was twenty-six when she could get married without obtaining her sister's consent.

Churchill also relieved Princess Margaret of her role of regent by a new Regency Act introduced in 1953. This named Prince Philip as regent and not 'the person, twenty-one years or older, who was next in succession to the throne. . . .' In retrospect it seems very sensible to have the father of the future monarch as regent. This view was expressed by the Queen in the message which was read to the Commons by the Home Secretary, Sir David Maxwell-Fyfe (later Lord Kilmuir). The Queen wrote:

> *The uncertainty of human life leads me to put you in mind of the possibility that a child of myself and my dear husband may succeed to the throne whilst under the age of eighteen years. And I would recommend to your consideration whether it be not expedient to provide that, in that event and also in the event of a Regency becoming necessary during my lifetime, whilst there is no child or grandchild of ours who can be the Regent, my husband should be the Regent and be charged with the guardianship of the person of the Sovereign.*

On 14 November 1966 Prince Charles had his eighteenth birthday and thus obviated the possibility of his father ever becoming regent. From that date Charles was legally old enough to be crowned King in the event of his mother's death. He also became eligible to serve as a counsellor of state during any periods of absence or illness when the Queen might be unable to play her role as sovereign. Under an Act passed in 1943 the other counsellors of state are 'the wife or husband of the Sovereign and the four persons next in line of succession to the throne'. On Prince Charles' eighteenth birthday the other Counsellors were Prince Philip, the Queen Mother (specifically appointed under the Regency Act of 1953), Princess Margaret and the Duke of Gloucester.

None of this appeared in the court circular for 14 November, which simply noted: 'Today is the anniversary of the birthday of the Prince of Wales.' The BBC played the national anthem before early morning news programmes; the judges of the Central Criminal Court wore their scarlet robes in honour of the heir's birthday. But at Gordonstoun it was very much an ordinary day, although Charles received telephone calls from members of his family. Having broken his nose playing rugger, he was excused afternoon games, but he had his prep to do, his trumpet to play and duties to perform at Windmill Lodge, of which he was now helper, the Gordonstoun word for captain.

He was so successful in this role that in January 1967, in his penultimate term at the school, he was promoted to guardian, the head boy of the whole school. In this

Charles' last day at Gordonstoun. The Queen delighted pupils, parents and guests when she kissed her son on both cheeks as soon as they met.

position Charles acted as link between headmaster, housemasters and the boys. He had to see that the boys carried out the duties he listed for them or which were imposed on them by the school organization. Whenever necessary he had to act as spokesman for the boys before the staff. In carrying out the duties of this office he showed that his Australian venture had made him develop into a confident young man, willing and able to fulfil the various tasks of his new role with ease, and in such a way as to win the respect of both boys and staff.

On his eighteenth birthday Charles received an increase in his personal income. When he became Duke of Cornwall in 1952 he was entitled, under the Civil List Act of 1952, to one-ninth of the annual net revenue of the duchy of Cornwall, then totalling about £112,000. Just after Charles became eighteen Squadron-Leader Checketts, who had been his guardian-companion while he was in Australia, was appointed his equerry with an office at Buckingham Palace. In time to come Prince Charles would have to recruit secretaries, servants and so on, all of whose salaries would be paid for out of the Duke of Cornwall's income.

The future of the Prince of Wales naturally aroused wide interest at this time. In the aftermath of the Aberfan landslide tragedy in October 1966 some people asked that the Prince of Wales should become, in very deed, a Prince living in Wales. It was not clear what they expected him to do if he went, as they proposed, to live in Harlech or Caernarvon. Others wondered what was to become of the Prince, given that his mother was young and would, it was hoped, reign for many years to come.

The Queen and Prince Philip had already given thought to this situation. On 22 December 1965 they held a private dinner at Buckingham Palace for a group of five men who had been selected and brought together to discuss the future education of the Prince of Wales. They were the Archbishop of Canterbury, Dr Ramsay; Sir Charles Wilson, Principal of Glasgow University and Chairman of the Committee of Vice-Chancellors; the Prime Minister, Harold Wilson, who had gone via scholar-ships from an elementary school to Oxford where, like Sir Charles, he had taken a first-class honours degree in philosophy, politics and economics; the Dean of Windsor, Dr Robin Woods, who, in his two years at Windsor, had become a confi-dential friend and adviser to the royal family – his brother was Archbishop of Melbourne in whose diocese stood Geelong School; and Earl Mountbatten, 'Uncle Dickie', a valued and experienced adviser and one of the Battenberg brothers who had looked after Prince Philip in his early days. After dinner the hosts and their guests discussed what sort of education Prince Charles ought to receive once he left school. Not surprisingly Earl Mountbatten advocated that the young Prince should follow him and Prince Philip by joining the navy. Charles' grandfather, George VI, had also served in the navy before going to Cambridge. The 'grand committee' eventually agreed that the heir to the throne ought to go to a university before joining one of the armed services.

When it came to the question of choosing which university the Prince should attend sound arguments were voiced in favour of several of them. Balmoral is Charles' favourite among the royal homes and he has a Scottish grandmother. One of the four ancient Scottish universities would have seemed very suitable, but against this was the fact that by the time he left Gordonstoun to go to university he would already have spent nearly five years in Scotland. Given that the Queen had broken with tradition by sending him to school with other children, and had sent him to Gordonstoun and not a traditional public school, it was argued by others that she should maintain this attitude and allow Prince Charles to go to one of the new redbrick universities which have sprung up in post-war Britain. But the Prince himself has always shown a great interest in tradition. At Gordonstoun he had been obliged to live in a very untraditional community which offered him none of those links with the past which he has always treasured. So it seemed fair that he should be given the chance of going to one of the older universities, which narrowed the choice to Oxford or Cambridge. By the time he came back from Australia he had let it be known that he preferred Cambridge, which is not too far from Sandringham, is the university to which his fondly remembered grandfather had gone, and where he had visited his cousins, the two Gloucester boys.

There remained only for him to decide which college he would attend. Once again the Queen called on Dr Woods for his advice. He was asked to visit Cambridge during Michaelmas Term 1966 and consult the Vice-Chancellor and some heads of colleges before advising the Queen as to which seemed the most suitable of the colleges. After much discussion Dr Woods recommended that the Prince should become a student at Trinity, the largest of the Cambridge colleges. It had been founded in 1546 by Henry VIII 'to the glory and honour of Almighty God and the Holy and Undivided Trinity for the establishment of true religion and the extirpation of heresy and the education of youth in piety, virtue, discipline and learning'. It was the college to which Edward VII and George VI had gone as undergraduates. In 1967 its Master was Lord Butler, formerly a Conservative minister. Women had just started to be admitted into the college, which takes about half of its undergraduates from grammar schools; the Prince would have a chance to mix with students from a wide cross-section of society – he would, indeed, 'meet the people'.

On Sunday 4 December 1966 it was announced that 'the Prince of Wales has been accepted by Trinity College, Cambridge, for entry in October 1967'. How far that had really been fixed at the 1965 meeting cannot be known. But in *Majesty* Robert

Lacey's account of that meeting contains an interesting passage: '. . . It was Harold Wilson who suggested that Mountbatten should have the floor. "Ma'am, Dickie has not spoken yet," he said. "Can we have his opinion?" And so Lord Mountbatten proposed the formula that came to be adopted. "Trinity College like his grandfather, Dartmouth like his father and grandfather, and then to sea in the Royal Navy ending up with a command of his own."'

With the news there also appeared the text of an interview between Gower Jones, a journalist from the Press Association, and Prince Philip:

Mr Jones: *What were the considerations that prompted the Queen and your Royal Highness to choose a university education for the Prince of Wales?*
Prince Philip: *Well, primarily his own inclination. It's not a question of being told what he is to do. All the way through we've tried to explain to him what the situation is, what the possibilities are, and tried to make him feel that he was just as much involved in the choice of his education as we were. I think apart from that the alternatives were basically whether he was to go to university or whether he was to go into one of the Services. This was obviously a matter which to a certain extent depended on his choice – he was keen to go to university so we tried to figure out some way in which we could do this provided he was more or less qualified.*
Mr Jones: *What part in this decision did the dinner party at Buckingham Palace a year ago, attended by the Prime Minister, the Archbishop of Canter-bury, Admiral of the Fleet Earl Mountbatten of Burma, Professor Sir Charles Wilson and the Dean of Windsor, play in the decision?*
Prince Philip: *Well, it played its part to this extent. Knowing what he wanted, and knowing also that we agreed, what we wanted very much was to make sure that this idea commended itself to those people, particularly because we felt that in his particular position we wanted to make sure that they agreed that, even if he perhaps wasn't 100 per cent qualified, they would still think it was worthwhile his going to university considering what he was almost inevitably going to do. And the other thing was that we wanted their opinion as to the sort of programme that he ought to undertake. In other words, whether he ought to do a regular university course with a view to taking a specific degree, or whether it would be more valuable to him, again in his rather special position, to take a more generalized course without necessarily taking a specific and regular degree, but undertaking a course of instruction which would be equivalent to a degree course but not in the formal sense. It obviously entered our minds that if he had spent part of his school education abroad in a Commonwealth country, whether perhaps the course at*

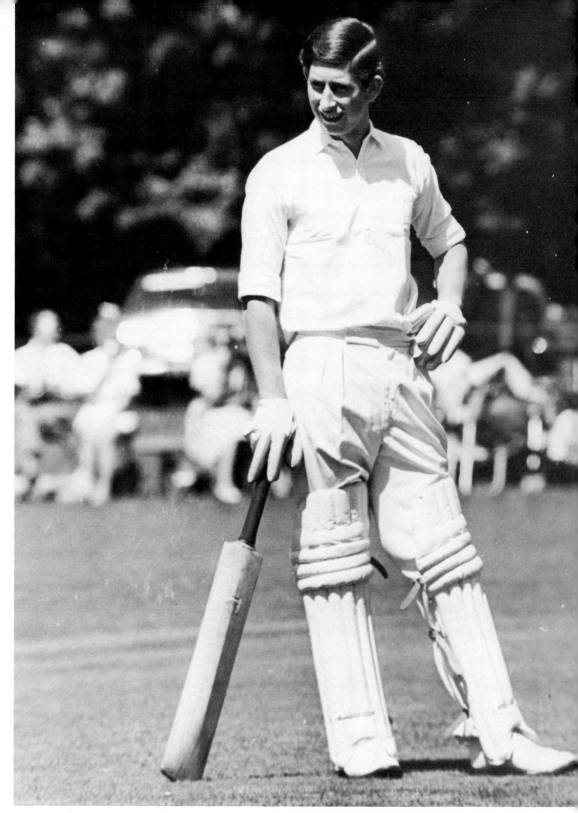

Playing cricket at Mersham Hatch.

university should include a period in a Commonwealth university. This again would have made it very difficult to have pursued a specific subject. This is slightly in the future. Then, of course, we discussed in a general way the pros and cons of, let's say, an older university, one of the new universities, the associations which they would have, the practical problems that they might raise, and so on. It was a very general discussion. As I see it now, there are three kinds of universities; there are the old universities, there are the 'red brick' universities, and the new universities. We discussed this at great length, and in the end we came to the conclusion that it is so difficult to choose between any of the new universities, and that particular associations which existed between one or another were so marginal that the consensus of opinion was that it should be one of the older ones. And Cambridge, I think, suggested itself for a number of reasons. His cousins had been there, his grandfather had been there, and East Anglia is relatively close to Sandringham, and in a sense all reasonable arguments seemed to point to Cambridge.

Mr Jones: *What are the Prince's qualifications for acceptance by the university?*

Prince Philip: *He's now taking two 'A' level subjects, History and French, and on his 'O' level performance and everything that we hear about his progress, both here and in Australia, there's no reason to suppose that he won't qualify in the ordinary course of events. On top of that there is, I think, some form of entrance examination, but this is really largely a matter for the individual colleges.*

Mr Jones: *What will Prince Charles be reading?*

Prince Philip: *Again, this isn't definite. I imagine that, having taken history, he will continue to take history. But we haven't worked out in detail what the course is to be. But we hope very much that it will include a number of fringe subjects and things which it will be valuable for him to have studied, rather than that he should become an academic historian. I think this is the important part. I think so much of the university programmes are geared to specialities, people who want to come out as specialists, who want to have a professional job. I think whatever he does there, it's more important, it seems to me, that he should have a broad base of instruction.*

Mr Jones: *Does this mean that the Prince would not have the opportunity of sitting for a degree?*

Prince Philip: *No, I wouldn't say that at all, but I'm not prepared to predict. What I want to make clear is that I don't think the course should be constrained in such a way because of the absolute need to take a degree. There isn't all that advantage in it.*

Mr Jones: *How long will Prince Charles be there?*

70

Looking like any other student,
Charles cycles past King's College,
Cambridge, book in hand.

Relaxing with fellow students outside a cave in Jersey during an archaeological study tour of the island.

Prince Philip: *I would assume the total length of his university period, whether here or abroad, would not be longer than normal, about three years.*
Mr Jones: *Are there any plans for a Commonwealth or overseas university afterwards?*
Prince Philip: *There are no plans, but this is obviously a possibility.*
Mr Jones: *After university, might the Prince have a period in the Royal Navy or some other Service?*
Prince Philip: *Well, I think, again without committing him or anybody else in any way, it would seem both natural and needful to him to have had some Service experience, I think either by doing a longish experience in one Service or by doing attachments to all three; I think this is a valuable experience, and it would be very useful to him in later life. Mind you, all this is not going to take all that amount of time. There'll be plenty of time for him to do other things afterwards.*
Mr Jones: *Is Prince Charles looking forward to going up to Cambridge?*
Prince Philip: *Well, yes, I think he's looking forward to leaving school. There comes a moment when you've had enough of it. . . .*

In October, Prince Charles took up residence in a second-floor room in New Court, which had been built in 1823. After Gordonstoun this must have appeared almost luxurious, although his small suite was merely a bedroom with an iron bed, a desk, cupboard and washbasin, and a sitting-room with a couple of chairs, a table, a sofa and a gas ring. His room opened on to a winding staircase, off which were a number of other rooms – a layout designed to encourage a sense of community among the inhabitants, so that Lord Butler's hope would be more easily fulfilled: 'The important thing when he first arrives is to find young friends who will take him out. The danger is sitting in a room all alone and doing nothing. It is far better to go out to a pub with friends and have a drink.' Prince Philip hoped that the press would find Cambridge 'a little bit more inaccessible' – Lord Butler, whose college suffered from the constantly increasing number of tourists even before the arrival of the Prince of Wales, said: 'We are inundated with visitors during the summer months. Great Court looks like the San Marco piazza at Venice and they glue their noses to the windows and peer in.'

Queen Victoria's son, later Edward VII, had gone to university accompanied by an over-protective but incompetent private tutor so that, as the *Daily Mirror* reported: 'Bertie . . . proved himself to be a well-dressed, amiable dolt.' The last Prince of Wales, later the Duke of Windsor, had, according to the *Mirror*, 'forged his reputation as a gay blade at Oxford,' and his social life at Magdalen 'was a pot-pourri of beagling, polo and roulette'. Charles was neither dolt nor gay blade. He had earned

Charles plays a singing dustman in a Cambridge revue called *Revulution*. He acted in several such revues during his three years at university: they provided ample opportunities for the Prince to display a variety of talents and a good-natured willingness to 'take the micky' out of himself and his position.

his place by gaining his 'A' level passes. He quickly settled down to work at Cambridge, seeming to revel in a student's week of nine lectures and ample time for individual work. He read widely and quickly, showed that he was well able to assimilate knowledge and interpret the information he acquired. During his first year he read for the archaeology and anthropology tripos but then switched to the history honours course. Like every student, he had a tutor to guide him and assist him with any difficulties in his personal life. Charles' tutor was Dr D.M. Marrian, an organic chemist – maybe a last, lingering attempt to give the future monarch some interest in science.

However, his interests had already taken shape during his earlier formative years and had been confirmed by his experiences at Gordonstoun and in Australia. This explains his choice of courses. He made a decision early in his undergraduate life that, like the rest of the student body, he would take examinations and obtain a bachelor's degree. There was obviously no need for him to take the examinations nor to obtain a degree; he was not, after all, going to need a job after graduating. But he felt that the examinations would provide him with something to aim at. The need to study in an organized way would provide him also with the framework needed to obtain the full benefit from his time at Cambridge.

So it was that he worked his way through the three years at Cambridge, wearing baggy corduroy trousers and sports jacket, his tousled hair even more unruly as he rode around the city on his bicycle. He did not join any of the more socially prestigious societies nor indulge in any of the hectic socializing that went on, as his princely predecessors had done. He did allow himself the luxury of an MGB sports car, although for the first year it had to be left outside the town since university regulations forbid freshmen to have their own cars in the town itself. In a college play he took the part of a vicar and had a custard pie slammed in his face. In a college revue, *Revulution*, he had the chance to display a variety of talents in pieces designed to encourage him to take the mickey out of himself and his position. As a Cockney dustman he stood in a dustbin and sang; in imitation of his favourites, the Goons, he adopted pidgin Indian and Chinese accents. But he got the best applause for two sketches, in one of which he stepped on to the stage alone to remark: 'I lead a sheltered life,' and in another said: 'I like to give myself airs.' Charles joined in debates at the Union, continued to practise his cello, and played polo so well that the captain of the Cambridge team described him as 'the best player here'.

In 1958 the Queen had bestowed on her son the title of Prince of Wales. This automatically made him a Knight of the 'most noble and amiable company of St George named the Garter', which is the oldest order of chivalry in Britain. But it

Practising the cello: Charles has always been a keen cellist, and has taken part in a
number of concerts.

was not until June 1968 that Charles was officially installed as a member of the Order, whose members meet each June at Windsor Castle. Here, in the throne room, the new Knight was invested by the Queen who buckled the blue and gold garter on his left leg while the Bishop of Winchester proclaimed:

> *To the honour of God Omnipotent, and in Memorial of the Blessed Martyr, Saint George, tie about thy leg, for thy Renown, this Most Noble Garter. Wear it as the symbol of the Most Illustrious Order never to be forgotten or laid aside, that hereby thou mayest be admonished to be courageous, and having undertaken a just war, into which thou shalt be engaged, thou mayest stand firm, valiantly fight, courageously and successfully conquer.*

The future monarch swore an oath of loyalty to the Queen and promised to be faithful to the ideals of the Order, as his mother fixed his riband and star and placed the mantle and collar over his shoulder. Then the new Knight took lunch with the Queen and the other members of the Order. After lunch, dressed in blue velvet and his plumed hat, his large blue Garter insignia on his left breast, he took part in the procession to St George's Chapel. Every year this procession draws a vast crowd. In 1968 the crowds were thicker than usual since it was known that the newly installed Prince would be among the Knights. The introverted Charles looked a little embarrassed as he walked slowly in his new garb. It was perhaps a good rehearsal for that even greater public ordeal that he had yet to face at his installation as Prince of Wales at Caernarvon.

In the summer term of 1969 Prince Charles left Cambridge for a term's study at Aberystwyth University. This break in his normal course was needed, it was felt, to introduce him more fully to Wales and the Welsh language. Some saw it as a sop to the vociferous Welsh Nationalists; most Welsh people saw it as an honest attempt by 'Carlo bach' to equip himself better for his role as Prince of Wales. The Welsh Office in Whitehall was then in the charge of a Welsh-speaking minister, Cledwyn Hughes. He had encouraged the Prince to use some of his summer holidays before he went to Cambridge to read up the history, customs and culture of Wales. He also helped him acquire a little knowledge of the Welsh language – sufficient at least for him to pronounce the commoner place-names and the words he would have to use at his investiture.

There was a real fear that some of the more violent extremists among the Nationalists might make serious trouble, for they regarded Charles as the English usurper of the Welsh title. During a radio interview Prince Charles said:

Charles, having just been invested as a Knight of the Garter, walks in the procession with his grandmother.

I expect at Aberystwyth there may be one or two demonstrations, and as long as I don't get covered too much in egg and tomato I'll be all right, but I don't blame people demonstrating like that. They've never seen me before, they don't know what I'm like. I've hardly been to Wales, and you can't really expect people to be over-zealous about the fact of having a so-called English Prince to come amongst them and be frightfully excited. Once I've been there for eight weeks things might improve.

A lunatic fringe of the Nationalist movement, giving itself the title of the Free Wales Army, announced plans for his assassination. A strict security net was put in and around Aberystwyth with over seventy detectives living in the town, some enrolling as students at the university, so that they could keep a closer eye on him and on the activities of the leaders of the Nationalist movement among the student body. But from the beginning the new student, enrolled simply as 'Windsor, C.', was made welcome by the townspeople and the majority of students. Charles had a room in a hall of residence halfway up the hill overlooking the town and the sea. His tutor, Edward Millward, a fervent Nationalist, taught the Prince to speak Welsh and also gave him instruction in the history and culture of which the Welsh are rightly proud. Charles had earlier shown that, in spite of Cledwyn Hughes' encouragement and his own reading, he had little knowledge of Welsh history. When confronted by a gang of heckling Nationalists he had tried to talk to them, asking who was being commemorated by the banners which carried the name 'Llywelyn'. He had apparently not heard of the great Llywelyn, the last Welsh Prince of Wales who had sat alongside Edward III in the English Parliament and whose name is a rallying cry for Welsh Nationalists.

However Charles' easy charm, quiet diffidence and obvious desire to please won him many friends, and the protests of the minority died away within a few weeks of his arrival. Every day there was a small crowd of women, armed only with shopping bags, waiting at the entrance to the hall of residence or at the college gates, hoping to catch a glimpse of the young Prince. On some days the college porter would announce that 'the Prince will not be down today', and the crowd would melt away, disappointed at having been deprived of its peep show. One of Charles' strong points was his sense of humour – he allowed himself to be used in parades and charades through the town. After only a few weeks at the college the future monarch addressed the National Eisteddfod of the Urdd meeting in Aberystwyth. He made a five-minute speech in Welsh which won the approval not only of the people at the Eisteddfod but also of the majority of the inhabitants of the town, most of whom are Welsh-speaking.

On 17 May 1967 the Queen announced her decision to invest the Prince of Wales at Caernarvon Castle in the summer of 1969, by which time he would have completed two years of his degree course. This gave everyone time to prepare for the elaborate ceremonies which were to take place. As the announcement said: 'Her Majesty has commanded the Duke of Norfolk, as Earl Marshal, to co-ordinate the arrangements for the installation ceremony in consultation with the Secretary of State for Wales and the Constable of Caernarvon Castle.'

The Constable of Caernarvon Castle was Lord Snowdon, husband of Princess Margaret and therefore Charles' uncle. It was at Caernarvon that the last Prince of Wales had been invested in 1911, when the chief organizer of the ceremonies had been the Chancellor of the Exchequer, the ebullient David Lloyd George. Ironically, his daughter, Lady Megan Lloyd George, a member of the Labour Party, had recently been defeated in a by-election at Carmarthen by the president of the Welsh Nationalist Party, Gwynfor Evans. When asked for his comments on the announce-ment of the investiture, the new MP said:

> Of course, this is a tremendous honour for Prince Charles, but I can't help thinking of the original purpose for giving the male Heir to the English Crown the title Prince of Wales. It had been a powerful and emotive title in Welsh history and, following the two hundred years' struggle of the Welsh against the Norman-English order, it was taken by Edward I and given to his eldest son in order to weaken Welsh resistance and to pave the way for integrating the Welsh nation in the English state. Not unnaturally I am unenthusiastic about this. The situation would be quite different if Wales had Commonwealth status, in which case the Queen of England would be the Queen of Wales, as she is the Queen of Canada, Australia and New Zealand when she goes to those countries.

In 1967 Charles accompanied his parents to the State Opening of Parliament. His father sat on the consort's throne while his mother read the Queen's speech from the sovereign's throne. As Charles gazed out over the massed ranks of lords religious and secular, and the officers of Parliament in their strange garb, the thought must have crossed his mind that in time the task of reading that speech would be his. Early in 1969 he assumed another role when he became Colonel-in-Chief of the newly-formed Regiment of Wales, whose uniform he wore at his investiture at Caernarvon.

Ever since the Queen had announced a date for the investiture ceremony there had been a flurry of Nationalist activity, threats to the lives of the Prince and his parents and the development of such a degree of tension that at one point there was serious discussion about cancelling the ceremony. According to a survey carried out for the *Western Mail* in September 1968 by the Opinion Research Centre, forty-four per cent of Welsh people thought that the investiture was a waste of money. However, the Welsh-speaking Secretary of State for Wales, George Thomas, argued that the show had to go on, since the government and the crown must not be seen to be cowed by the threats of the Nationalists. Indeed, it was argued that the investiture would be a way of attacking the claims of the Nationalists to speak for the Welsh people. In February 1969 Prince Philip was interviewed on television. About the possibilities of the investiture being cancelled, he said: 'I think the doubts are not so much allow-ing him to take part at all, but if we had any doubts, perhaps to what extent this sort of virtually mediaeval revival was relevant, and I think that probably the final governing factor was that it was quite obvious that a very large proportion of Welsh opinion favoured this. This really tipped the scales.'

There seemed a good deal of uncertainty about the truth of that last princely claim. Plaid Cymru, the Nationalist party which had 40,000 members, decided to ignore the investiture. Some vented their anger in painting out English names on road signs; graffiti-minded patriots daubed bridges and walls with anti-English and anti-monarchy slogans; cartoons were widely distributed in which the young Prince was made to appear as a lapdog. The pop-song *Carlo, Carlo* went to the top of the Welsh hit parade:

> *I have a friend who lives in Buckingham Palace*
> *And Carlo Windsor is his name*
> *The last time I went round to his house*
> *His mother answered the door and said:*
> *'Carlo, Carlo, Carlo is playing polo today*
> *Carlo is playing polo with his Dadd.'*
> *So come all ye serfs of Wales and join in the chorus*
> *At last you have a prince in the land of song.*

But more serious than these demonstrations of antipathy to the monarchy was the outbreak of bomb attacks which began on 17 November 1967, when 400 Welshmen assembled in the Temple of Peace in Cardiff's civic centre to make arrangements for the ceremony. The Free Wales Army planted a bomb at the Temple, which ex-ploded, causing £30,000 worth of damage, though no one was injured. Before the investiture day there were twelve further bomb attacks on government buildings, pipelines taking water from Welsh valleys to English cities, an RAF station and the headquarters of the police and the electricity board in Cardiff.

Nine members of the Free Wales Army were arrested in February; their trial lasted from 16 April to 1 July, the day of the investiture, when two of them were sentenced to fifteen months' imprisonment. The long trial served to enhance the reputation of

Smiles of pride and relief from the Queen and Prince Charles after his investiture as Prince of Wales at Caernarvon Castle.

this small army and also increased the tension in royal circles. Helicopters were on constant patrol guarding the many pipelines; several thousand policemen were brought into Caernarvon; the castle was regularly searched in case explosives had been planted and tight security was maintained during the preparations for the cere-mony. On the very morning of the investiture, two terrorists handling a badly made bomb blew themselves up in their attempt to attack the local government offices at Abergele, only thirty-five miles away from Caernarvon. Great care was therefore paid to security. The royal train bringing the royal family from London was halted while a hoax bomb was dismantled under a bridge outside Chester; policemen in rubber dinghies patrolled the Menai Straits; in Caernarvon the police watched the swelling crowds with the aid of overhead TV cameras. In spite of all this, however, a bomb exploded while the Prince was travelling in a motorcade to the castle. Several of the cars were damaged but no one was injured, and the show went on.

As Charles arrived at the castle the state trumpeters of the Household Cavalry sounded a salute, his personal banner was unfurled and as he walked to the Chamber-lain Tower the crowd sang *God Bless the Prince of Wales*. Meanwhile the Queen was being driven in her state coach drawn by its eight Windsor greys. A young man threw a banana skin under their hooves but failed to disrupt the royal progress. Lord Snowdon, as Constable of the Castle, surrendered its key to his sovereign who made her way to the centre of the arena. Here she told the Earl Marshal, the Duke of Norfolk, to send for the waiting Prince. He arrived, accompanied by heralds, the Secretary of State for Wales, and members of the House of Lords carrying the insignia with which he was to be invested. Prince Charles knelt before his mother, who handed the letters patent to the Home Secretary, James Callaghan, to read:

> *Elizabeth the Second by the Grace of God of the United Kingdom of Great Britain and Northern Ireland and of Our other Realms and Territories Queen Head of the Commonwealth Defender of the Faith. To All Lords Spiritual and Temporal and all other of Our Subjects whatsoever to whom these Presents shall come Greeting Know Ye that we have made and created by these Our Letters Do make and create Our most dear Son Charles Philip Arthur George Prince of the United Kingdom of Great Britain and Northern Ireland Duke of Cornwall and Rothesay Earl of Carrick Baron of Renfrew Lord of the Isles and Great Steward of Scotland PRINCE OF WALES and EARL OF CHESTER.*
>
> *And to the same Our most dear Son Charles Philip Arthur George have given and granted and by this Our Present Charter Do give grant and confirm the name style title dignity and honour of the same Principality and Earldom.*

And him Our most dear Son Charles Philip Arthur George as he has been accustomed We do ennoble and invest with the said Principality and Earldom by girding him with a Sword by putting a Coronet on his head and a Gold Ring on his finger and also by delivering a Gold Rod into his hand that he may preside there and may direct and defend those parts. To hold to him and his heirs Kings of the United Kingdom of Great Britain and Northern Ireland and of Our other Realms and Territories Heads of the Commonwealth for ever. Wherefore We will and strictly command for Us Our heirs and successors that Our most dear Son Charles Philip Arthur George may have the name style title dignity and honour of the Principality of Wales and Earldom of Chester aforesaid unto him and his heirs Kings of the United Kingdom of Great Britain and Northern Ireland and of Our other Realms and Territories Heads of the Commonwealth as are above mentioned. In Witness whereof We have caused these Our Letters to be made Patent. Witness Ourself at Westminster the twenty-sixth day of July in the seventh year of Our Reign.

While these phrases were being intoned, Charles was invested with his insignia of silver gilt sword, coronet, gold ring, mantle of purple velvet trimmed with an ermine cape, and long golden rod. There was a homely touch to the ceremony as he helped adjust the coronet while his mother fastened and straightened his mantle. After George Thomas had read the charter in Welsh the Prince knelt before the Queen to pay his homage: 'I, Charles Prince of Wales, do become your liege man of life and limb and of earthly worship, and faith and truth I will bear unto you to live and die against all manner of folks.'

After giving his mother the kiss of fealty Charles listened to a loyal address read in Welsh and English by the President of the University College of Aberystwyth, Sir Ben Bowen Thomas. Charles replied to the address, speaking first in English, then in Welsh. After a short religious ceremony the Prince was then taken to be presented, at three different points, to the cheering crowd. About forty per cent of British households watched the ceremony on television and the town of Caernarvon became a tourist centre. Prince Charles toured his principality and was rapturously received wherever he went by people who seemed anxious to wipe away the memories of the bombings, to ease the tensions and to show the future monarch that he was indeed welcome in the hills and valleys.

6

A Year of Service
and of Flying

1970

The period surrounding the investiture had been one of great emotional involvement for the young Charles, with his ideal of living up to his motto, '*Ich Dien*' (I serve), and his horror at the injury suffered by a young schoolboy when a booby trap exploded in Caernarvon. The boy had been playing football when the bomb went off, and had to have a leg amputated. The news saddened the idealistic young Prince who had summed up his conception of his position in a radio interview: 'I think that "I serve" is a marvellous motto, and I think it is the basis of one's job; to serve other people. If you have a sense of duty – and I like to think I have – then service is something that you give yourself to people, particularly if they want you and sometimes if they don't.' The Prince's own wish was to visit the young boy in hospital, but his doctors thought that this might over-excite the injured boy and delay his recovery. However the Prince wrote to express his sympathy for the 'cowardly and appalling hurt and harm'. When a fund was raised for the boy, Charles made a large contribution. It was against this sombre background to his memories of the investiture that he had a brief holiday with Princess Anne in Malta where, his friends realized, thoughts of the injured boy acted as a damper on the normally cheerful Prince.

After this short holiday the Prince returned to Trinity for his final year. He had a new set of rooms, on the south side of the Great Court, from which he could hear the famous chapel clock and the constant splashing of Nevill's fountain. His natural love for 'the things of the past' must have been at least partially satisfied with this environ-ment, while in his reflective manner he must often have thought of the other great men who had enjoyed the sights and sounds of the Great Court – poets as diverse as Dryden, Byron, Tennyson and Housman, historians and writers such as Macaulay and Thackeray and, more recently, the musician Vaughan Williams.

In November 1969 the Prince celebrated his twenty-first birthday. A number of

Charles poses at the controls of an aircraft for an unconventional twenty-first birthday portrait.

undergraduates climbed the rooftops of the buildings opposite Charles' rooms on the night of 13–14 November and put up a banner saying 'Happy Birthday, Charlie', which they hoped he would see when he got up in the morning. This was at once a public recognition of his popularity among his fellow undergraduates and of their appreciation of his sense of humour. However, the Prince was not in college. On 13 November he had had a flying lesson and had then gone on to London to spend his birthday at the Palace with his mother and father. Later he was to say of his family: 'I think of my family as very special people. I have never wanted not to have a home life – to get away from home. I love my home life. We happen to be a very close-knit family. I am happier at home with my family than anywhere else.' This is a reflection of the success of the Queen as a mother who had always taken care that, in spite of her public duties, she did not ignore her children.

Charles shares with his mother a sense of religious dedication to his role, which was evident in the investiture ceremony, and to his family on the morning of his birthday, when he got up early to go with Princess Anne and his beloved grandmother, the Queen Mother, to visit the Chapel Royal of St John in the Tower of London. Here, with no attendant publicity, the young Prince made 'an act of thanksgiving and dedication for his future life'.

In the evening a concert was given in the Palace ballroom. The music-loving Prince had invited Yehudi Menuhin and his Bath Festival orchestra to play a programme that included a Mozart violin concerto and, his own special choice, a Haydn cello concerto. There were about 400 guests at the concert and the festivities which followed. These included fireworks in the garden of the Palace after which, said one report: 'most older people, the shoals of ambassadors, left. . . .' The younger guests were entertained by a pop group in the Music Room. About 150 people danced until the early hours; breakfast was served at three o'clock. The Queen, no doubt proud of her son and more than pleased with the way in which he had grown into manhood, stayed up to enjoy the evening. Her natural high spirits, which have to be held in check in her public role, were allowed freer rein and, according to one reputable observer, she kicked off her shoes the better to join in the dancing.

During the spring term 1970, Prince Charles had to begin final preparations for his degree examination while also undertaking a number of public duties. Now that he was twenty-one his mother and father wanted to bring him forward as a member of the 'royal firm'. On 11 February 1970 the Prince of Wales was introduced into the House of Lords. Princesses Anne, Margaret and Alexandra led a large Palace party to see the young Prince, decked in his peer's scarlet robe, ermine-collared and with four rows of ermine and gold, take his place as a member of the Lords. They watched, along with the lords and bishops crowding the benches as, for the first time, the Prince's crown was carried in state into Parliament. There had been an un- precedently high demand for seats in the various galleries – from wives of members of the Lords, from the general public and from ambassadors and other representatives of foreign governments. Because the number of places in the galleries was limited a ballot was held, and the lucky winners saw the Duke of Kent and the Duke of Beaufort, sponsors for the new member, lead him into the chamber of the House. They watched as he doffed his velvet tricorne hat three times, bowing each time to the empty throne. They heard him pledge loyalty to his mother – and to himself – at the table in the Chamber: 'I, Charles, Prince of Wales, do swear by Almighty God that I will be faithful and bear true allegiance to Her Majesty Queen Elizabeth, her heirs and successors, so help me God.' His family may have already known that some, at least, of this ceremony would appeal to Charles' sense of the ridiculous. Later he would talk of his temporary fantasy as he stood in his robes and tricorne hat; for a moment he felt like a town crier and he had to stop himself cupping his hands to his mouth and yelling: 'Oyez, Oyez'.

This sense of the ridiculous feeds on a fertile imagination. Those who knew him well had always been aware of this; people who served with him in the RAF or Royal Navy were to learn about it first-hand. The wider public was given a glimpse of it when, during an interview, Charles talked about the day he was in attendance while his mother launched a new ship for the Royal Navy. As the ship slid down the slip- way he had a vision of the top brass all slipping gently along with the ship. He imagined that he heard himself giving a commentary: 'They're disappearing. They're waving. All that's left on the water is a couple of flowered hats and a bowler hat.' It comes as no surprise that this imaginative Prince is a fan of the Goons and took great pleasure in reviewing Harry Secombe's autobiography.

In April 1970, as yet another step along the road to a fuller public life, the Prince was sworn in as a member of the Queen's Privy Council. When monarchs effectively ruled as well as reigned, the Council was the sovereign's personal council. Even today the Privy Council remains, in theory, the foremost constitutional body; all members of the cabinet have to be sworn in as members of the Council before being allowed to take up their cabinet post. Privy Councillors enjoy the style of 'The Right Honourable' and they are appointed for life. There are therefore a large number of Privy Councillors who in theory are entitled to attend Council meetings. In fact, and by custom, only members of the government of the day attend normal meetings and this is on the invitation of the Lord President of the Council – who is always a member of the cabinet of the day. The full Council comes together on the death of one sovereign to swear allegiance to the new sovereign. The smaller, politically con- trolled Council meets about ten times each year. The 'Queen in Council' has the right to declare war or to make peace, although in fact this right only exists because the Council's decisions are those of the cabinet which has the support of a parliamentary majority.

As a member of the Council Prince Charles has been brought more closely into contact with the process of government. The theoretical lessons learned have all been reinforced by personal experience – the best teacher. Once again the guiding hand of his mother has been instrumental in ensuring that her heir will not be as unprepared for his role as were the future Edward VII, George V and George VI.

Queen Elizabeth the Queen Mother had been a great help to George VI when he became King after his brother abdicated in 1936. She had shared Queen Mary's anger at Edward VIII's failure to accept the duties of his position and blamed him for the relatively early death of George VI. The present Queen, as head of the royal family, went out of her way to try to heal the breach between the Duke of Windsor and other members of royalty. While the Queen Mother refused to allow the Duchess of Windsor to attend George VI's funeral in 1952, and the Duke himself would not bring his wife to Queen Mary's funeral in 1953, Queen Elizabeth visited the Duke and Duchess when they came to London for the Duke to undergo an eye operation, sent him a telegram on his seventieth birthday in 1964, and insisted that younger members of the royal family visited the Windsors whenever they were in Paris. In 1966 the Windsors rode in the official procession to the unveiling of a commemorative plaque to Queen Mary. This was the first official and public recognition of the Duchess by the monarch, who also persuaded her mother to talk to the Windsors at the reception which followed the unveiling. In the autumn of 1969 the Queen took her newly invested son on a private visit to Paris and the Windsors so that he could meet the previous Prince of Wales. Charles, as future head of the royal family, may have to show similar breadth of outlook and a high degree of Christian charity in the event of future estrangements. If he is ever called upon to act as peacemaker he will have the advantage of having seen his mother at work in that role.

The newly installed member of the House of Lords was taken to Strasbourg in February 1970 by his father. Here they attended a Council of Europe conference on conservation. The Prince of Wales had already shown a keen interest in the problems of conservation, playing an active part in the presentation of a film on rural Wales and writing an article, 'The Living World of Animals', for *Reader's Digest*, so it was fitting that he should give his support to an international conference on conservation.

The visit to Strasbourg gave Prince Philip the chance of a meeting with his sisters, Margarita and Sophie. Their mother, Princess Alice of Greece, had died at Buckingham Palace just before Christmas 1969 and this was the first reunion, since that sad occasion, of what Charles refers to as the 'other family'. While Philip enjoyed seeing his sisters, Charles met his German cousins – Prince Guelf and Prince George of Hanover (who had been at Gordonstoun), their younger sister Princess Frederica, and an older half-sister, Princess Clarissa. Guelf, only a little older than Charles, was already married and to a commoner, something which had offended some people with a strong attachment to courtly practice and ancient precedent. Those journalists who spotted a love match whenever they saw Charles with a possible bride noted with alacrity that Princess Clarissa was 'only' three years older than Charles, that her visits to Windsor were marked by the insertion of her name in the court circular, and described her as the ideal bride. This, they claimed, was a relationship on the Victoria and Albert lines; they, too, had been first cousins, one had been German-born while the other was the English sovereign. When the Princess married a French commoner in 1971 the journalists were temporarily disappointed but went on, undeterred, with their match-making prophecies.

Meanwhile the student Prince was busy with his studies, and, during the spring term of 1970, with playing a part in a revue presented by the Dryden Society under the title *Quiet Flows the Don*, an allusion to academics and a pun on the famous Russian novel. Although Charles had precious little time to spare he played in twenty-five of the thirty scenes in the revue, which ran for a week. The Queen and Princess Anne went to see the show one evening, after dining with the Prince in his rooms at Great Court.

During the Easter vacation of 1970 Prince Charles flew to join his parents and Princess Anne, who were on a royal tour of New Zealand and Australia to celebrate the bicentennial of Captain Cook's voyage. This was the first royal visit to Australasia for seven years, and when Charles met his parents in Wellington, New Zealand, he entered wholeheartedly into the spirit of the tour 'as though his life depended on it', according to one friend. During this tour the Queen introduced that note of informality which has been given the nickname 'the royal walkabout'. The crowds turned out in unexpectedly large numbers, in spite of the doomwatchers who had prophesied that the welcome in New Zealand and Australia would be cooler than it had been in the past; the Australians and New Zealanders, it was claimed, were too sophisticated to be taken in by the glamour and tinsel as their parents had been; the spirit of republicanism, it was predicted, would show itself very clearly. In fact the welcome was warmer than ever; the crowds seemed to want to say 'thank you' not only to the Queen and Prince Philip but also to the two royal children. As if in response to this, the Queen walked among the crowds, tramping over pavements, tracks and grasslands, chatting to hundreds of people. Prince Philip, Princess Anne and Prince Charles followed her example, Anne and Charles concentrating on talking to some of the many thousands of children and young people who gathered to see them along their route.

Charles watched his mother open the New Zealand Parliament on 13 March 1970; no doubt the ceremony deepened his awareness of the value of the Commonwealth. He watched a re-enactment of the landing by Captain Cook in 1770 at Slip Cove in Queen Charlotte's Sound. After New Zealand there followed, in early April, the tour of Australia. Charles said that he felt he was celebrating his 'homecoming', so much had he enjoyed his time at Timbertop. Prince Philip told the Prime Minister of New South Wales – Robin Askin – that Charles 'talks of feeling at home all the time'. At Canberra he played polo, at Bondi he went surf-riding and at Coogee Beach showed that he was well able to deal with some, at least, of the more inane among the sightseers. Two of them, alluding to his father's nationality, asked Charles if he could speak Greek. 'Yes, I can say "—— off,"' he replied. Reports of this exchange merely served to win him even more popularity and to heighten the interest in the royal tour. From Melbourne Charles took Princess Anne to see Timbertop. He spoke to a rally of young farmers, saying: 'That school's probably the reason why, whenever I come back to Australia, I experience a curious and inexplicable sensation that I belong.'

Charles left the tour to fly to Japan for the international Expo 70. He spent five days in Japan, his first mission on his own. He dined with Emperor Hirohito and in so doing helped to pave the way for the visit of the Queen and Prince Philip in 1975 to the country whose people had been a cruel enemy during World War II, and against whose forces his Uncle Dickie had waged a successful campaign as Supreme Commander South-east Asia in 1944 and 1945. Charles had a variety of tasks to perform during his short stay. He went on the early morning run of the 150-mph 'bullet train' from Tokyo to Kyoto, and undertook a series of visits to temples, castles and palaces in that ancient capital of Japan. He ate a meal using chopsticks, sitting stiff-backed for two hours on a straw mat in a restaurant. There was the well-advertised attendance of the geisha girl who massaged his back after lunch, and the well-rehearsed thanks in Japanese, '*Arigato! Arigato!*' At Expo 70 itself he visited twenty-one pavilions and exhibitions and played host to representatives of the seventy-seven nations exhibiting there. Among the guests was Mr Akio Morita, president of the giant Sony company. When the Prince found out that Sony was thinking of building a factory in Europe he suggested that the firm should look at sites in Wales. This royal interest can have played no little part in Sony's decision to build their new factory, which he had great pleasure in opening in 1974, in Glamorgan.

After Easter the Prince had to return to the realities of university life. Within a month of his visit to Japan he was undergoing the ordeal of final examinations. Along

Sharing a joke with his father and sister during their tour of the North-West Territories of Canada.

With the winner of a beauty contest in Yellowknife. Before the competition Charles had been asked if he would kiss the winner, and had replied: 'May I see her first, and may I choose where I kiss her?'

with his begowned peers he went to the Old Schools to answer six papers, each of three hours. The examination system precluded any favouritism – the papers were, as usual, anonymous and were marked without the examiners having any idea which papers were the Prince's. When we consider the many interruptions to the Prince's university life, it is all the more to his credit that he gained 'an average degree', becoming a Bachelor of Arts, class 2, division 2. One is entitled to wonder how much better he might have done if he had not had to cope with the official duties incumbent upon a member of the royal family. Even with these handicaps Prince Charles became the first heir to the throne to gain a degree, other than an honorary one. He had proved to himself, his family and the public at large that he was capable of hard, steady work and that he was well fitted to cope with the role that would one day be his.

Charles had spoken on the telephone to the Queen on her forty-fourth birthday while she was cruising on the royal yacht off the Great Barrier Reef. She was back in the Palace to receive the telephone call which he made after his examination results had been posted on the university notice-board. She shared his pleasure and pride. The Queen, Prince Philip and Princess Anne were off on another royal tour on 5 July, this time to visit the North-west Territories of Canada and the province of Manitoba, both of which were celebrating their centenaries in 1970 and neither of which had seen the Queen on her previous visit to Canada – curtailed because of the impending birth of Prince Andrew.

Charles flew out to join them, first visiting the Governor-General at Government House, Ottawa, and calling on Prime Minister Trudeau. Charles invited the Prime Minister's twenty-one-year-old niece, Jocelyne Rouleau, to accompany him on his rip to the north. On this visit to the Arctic regions they fished Eskimo-style through he ice at midnight in a fresh-water river, and the following morning enjoyed the catch of Arctic grayling at breakfast. At Tuktoyaktuk on the Arctic Ocean Charles and the rest of the family watched an Eskimo drum dance. At Yellowknife he attended a barbecue and was given a number of gifts – furs, ivory and a seascape. He was asked to kiss the winner of an Eskimo beauty contest, answering: 'May I see her first, and may I choose where I kiss her?' At Fort Smith a buffalo barbecue had been arranged; then they visited the mines at Pine Point before moving on to the final stage of the tour at Winnipeg, the capital of Manitoba. Here Charles, the country-lover, enjoyed a canoe trip along the Red River, a visit to a prairie horse show at Swan River and a trip by helicopter along the shores of Duck Bay.

When this visit was over, the Queen and Prince Philip flew back to London while Prince Charles and Princess Anne went down to Washington as guests of President and Mrs Nixon and their daughters, Tricia and Julie, and the latter's husband, David

Tricia Nixon explains the intricacies of American baseball to Prince Charles during a private, three-day visit to Washington with Princess Anne.

Meeting dancers who put on a display in Charles' honour in Fiji. The Prince was representing the Queen at Fiji's independence celebrations.

Eisenhower. Here, as in Germany, Charles was with people of his own age, for four days, in what he described publicly as 'a sensational climax' to his journey to North America. He was later to express bitter resentment at the way in which President Nixon's publicity team seemed to want to matchmake, with Tricia Nixon in the role of Princess Charming.

The visit to the Nixons was, supposedly, a private one. But for the royals a private visit is a rarity, particularly to a publicity-conscious President of the USA. There were trumpeters on the lawn of the White House, articles in the press comparing the Prince with his predecessor, the Duke of Windsor, and that other Prince of Wales, later Edward VII, who had stayed at the White House in 1860 during a more formal visit. Prince Charles, like Prince Edward, was taken down the Potomac River to visit George Washington's house and simple grave at Mount Vernon. As with Victoria's heir, so with Charles, who was accompanied by a mass of reporters and photographers, radio commentators and TV crews, all of whom made it difficult for the Prince to see much of the Washington home, described by Prince Edward in a letter to his father, Prince Albert: 'Mount Vernon is a much revered spot by the Americans . . . the house is unfortunately in very bad repair and falling into decay.'

In 1860 the Prince had visited the opera in Philadelphia where the audience rose spontaneously to sing *God Save the Queen*; in 1970, when Prince Charles and his sister paid an unscheduled visit to an open-air concert in Lafayette Park, the audience interrupted the performance with a storm of applause and the orchestra played one of Elgar's Pomp and Circumstance marches. In 1860 Prince Edward had met members of the Cabinet, military commanders who had won fame in Indian wars and who would, within a short time, be fighting in the bloody Civil War between North and South. In 1970 Charles met the first men on the moon, Neil Armstrong and Frank Bormann, who had already met other members of the royal family during a visit to Britain in 1969.

In October 1970 Charles, freed now from the pressure of study and not yet enrolled as a member of one of the armed services, represented the Queen at Fiji's independence celebrations. During the earlier royal tour the Queen, Prince Philip and Princess Anne had flown to Fiji in March 1970 to embark on the *Britannia* before making their way to New Zealand. They had also visited Tonga, and Anne's account of that section of the tour had made Charles regret that, because of his studies, he had been forced to miss it. Now, maybe as compensation for his earlier deprivation, Charles – as the senior member of the younger generation of royalty – went to Fiji. He remarked on the island's decision to remain inside the Commonwealth on achieving its independence, noting that: 'There must be something to be said for the Commonwealth after all.'

That same autumn Prince Charles was invited to address the annual meeting of the Institute of Directors at the Albert Hall. Over 5000 members of the Institute turn up each year for this prestigious gathering, at which a major figure is invited to make a keynote speech to the leaders of British industry and commerce. It was the largest and perhaps the most important gathering the Prince had ever addressed. He spoke for half an hour in an engaging style, and was described by one observer as 'pretending naïve ignorance and then speaking forcefully for his own generation.' Charles' speech included these words: 'Whoever invited me exploited my extreme ignorance. I assumed you were a small business organization. Little did I know that I had agreed to speak to five thousand whizz kids, tycoons, industrial giants. . . .' He told of his visit to the President of the U S A, his journey to Fiji where he had watched the hauling down of the Union Jack, the symbol of colonialism, but had rejoiced when Fiji immediately joined the Commonwealth. He spoke of a confrontation in Bermuda where an opposition party had referred to him as 'representing the forces of imperialism'. 'But,' he continued, 'the Commonwealth is a group of nations of mutual understanding concerning freedom and democracy. That by any standards is a jolly good start.' The critical and professional audience greeted his speech with 'a sustained applause', an accolade not easily given by such a gathering, one of whose members declared that it was 'like listening to one's own son'.

In November 1970 Charles celebrated his twenty-second birthday with another concert at the Palace; this time the programme included a cello concerto accompanied by the Welsh harpist, Ossian Ellis. Charles had long since overcome the shyness that had once been such an inhibiting factor; his studies, overseas journeys, official duties and public welcome had all contributed to making him a confident, though not brash, young man. He had retained and further developed his love for the countryside, for the Commonwealth, for music and for zany fun. He had visited Bermuda as part of that island's celebration of 350 years of parliamentary government. Addressing the gathering of politicians there, Charles remarked: 'Bearing in mind that I am the first Charles to have anything to do with a Parliament for 350 years, I might have turned nasty and dissolved you.' Charles shares this sense of fun with his mother who has, however, rarely felt free to indulge it publicly. Prince Philip has always been more outspoken, but Charles' humour is more kindly than the sharper, more biting wit of his father. This will stand him in good stead and make future royal speeches that much easier for both listener and reader.

In February 1971 he went on a two-week photographic and fishing safari in Kenya with Princess Anne, who was helping to make a *Blue Peter* children's television film for the Save the Children Fund. Charles was at the site of Treetops Lodge exactly nineteen years to the day on which his mother had received the news of her father's death. A fire had destroyed the wild fig tree and look-out post in its branches and a modern hotel now stood on the site. To visit this country and this place in particular had long been a dream of his, conscious as he was both of its significance for his mother and of its concern for animal conservancy with which he, too, was much involved.

While Princess Anne got on with her task of film-making, Charles and his equerry, David Checketts, went by air, bus and motorboat to a fishing lodge on Lake Rudolf from which he walked fifty miles on a four-day trek with pack-camels through the wild game reserve of Ngare Ndare. Charles had enjoyed living out of doors at Balmoral when he was a child, but living rough in Kenya was a far cry from peaceful nights in a sleeping bag at Balmoral. One night, awakened by the noise of panicking camels, he saw, about thirty yards away, a rhinoceros. Fortunately for him it merely snorted and walked away. This trip through the game park served to deepen his love for the outdoors, already a feature of his character and one previously heightened by his experiences at Gordonstoun and Timbertop. It also presented him with the sort of challenge which, he has said, he welcomes: 'I always feel that it is worthwhile challenging yourself and this is what I do most of the time. Perhaps to too great an extent sometimes. Perhaps I push myself too much. But this is my outlook on life.' He has also said that 'living dangerously tends to make you appreciate life much more'. While it would be foolish to exaggerate the dangers facing him in the Kenyan game park there is little doubt that life there, even if it was only for four days, was rougher and harder than life in his more normal and palatial surroundings.

As if in recognition of his increasing maturity an increasing number of calls were made on his time. He was invited to one of the weekly editorial lunches given by *Punch*, where he carved his initials on the editorial table. At a more dignified level, in March 1971 he was granted the Freedom of the City of London. The ceremony was held at the Guildhall to which he drove in an open landau through densely packed streets and cheering crowds. The young man who, a few days before, had lunched privately with the Prime Minister, Edward Heath, now went to lunch with the leading figures of the City of London who greeted him with a great ovation. Charles was wearing his uniform as Colonel-in-Chief of the Royal Regiment of Wales, together with the riband and star of the Order of the Garter. But the innate sense of fun showed through in the wide grin with which he listened to the reading of the declaration that he was the son of 'Prince Philip, Duke of Edinburgh, Citizen and Fishmonger of London and that he was born in lawful wedlock . . . his son so reputed and taken to be, and so they all say.'

It was a very confident young man who replied to the granting of the freedom scroll by the City Chamberlain, the aptly named Richard Whittington. This was the last

Unshaven but cheerful, Charles returns from four days of rough living in the Kenyan bush. He was on safari there with Princess Anne, who was helping to make a *Blue Peter* film for the Save the Children Fund.

public ceremony that Charles would undergo before entering the Royal Air Force. In his speech of thanks he referred to some criticism that had been made of the decision to enter one of the armed services:

> *It is pointless and ill-informed to say that I am entering a profession trained in killing. The services in the first place are there for fast, efficient and well-trained action in defence. Surely the services must attract a large number of duty-conscious people? Otherwise who else would subject themselves to being square-bashed, shouted at by petty officers and made to do ghastly things in force ten gales? I am entering the RAF and then the Navy because I believe I can contribute something to this country by so doing. To me it is a worthwhile occupation and one which I am convinced will stand me in good stead for the rest of my life.*

There was little surprise in the announcement that the Prince was to enter one of the armed services which came while he was still at Cambridge. His public reaction was: 'I am looking forward to it very much. I hope I shall not be too seasick.'

However, the plan was slightly changed to allow him to enter the RAF before he joined the Royal Navy. This was, in part, a recognition that this newest of the three services is, in a technological age, perhaps the most important. It was also an acknowledgement of the Prince's own pleasure in flying. While still an under-graduate at Cambridge he had taken flying lessons in a Chipmunk trainer at the RAF station at Oakington. Charles' own account of his first solo flight recalls his instructor saying, 'You're on your own, mate.' Then, said the Prince: 'I only had time for a few butterflies in the tummy. The moment I was in the air it was absolutely marvellous.' Early in 1970 he had done the forty hours' solo flying needed to gain a Grade A licence as a private pilot. He was fortunate in that the RAF had instituted a new system of graduate entry. In the old days all officer training had taken two and a half years. Now a degree was accepted as a substitute for the academic training given to officer cadets, and graduate entrants only required a one-year flying course before being eligible for their RAF wings. The enterprising Charles, however, already had sufficient flying time not to need that year's flying course and, by special dispensation, his course was shortened to five months which would enable him to enter the Royal Naval College, Dartmouth, in the autumn.

So it was an already commissioned flight-lieutenant who left Windsor in a heli-copter on 8 March 1971. At the RAF airfield at Benson he changed to a twin-engined Bassett in which he had done his flying for his pilot's licence, and flew on to the RAF College at Cranwell in Lincolnshire. Cranwell is a vast complex spread out over six square miles and includes airfields and parade grounds, engineering schools and shops, housing for about 4000 people and a central college block.

Charles being picked up by the Royal Marines after making his first parachute jump. He was the first member of the Royal Family to do so, and afterwards said it had been 'a hairy experience'.

Charles' much abbreviated course was packed and his progress through the highly organized scheme depended on his satisfactorily passing each stage. On 9 March he began an intensive ground school course during which he had to learn dinghy drill in the swimming-bath building, and landing drill in the gymnasium where he learned how to break the impact of a parachute landing. He attended technical sessions during which he learned about the aircraft he would fly and had to satisfy his instructors by answering test papers almost daily. There was air drill, ejector seat practice and more preparation for tests on aircraft problems.

It is a mark of the Prince's ability to cope with intensive work that he passed each stage of the course, and by the third Monday, 29 March, he went up for the first time in a Jet Provost; in April he was allowed to fly a Provost solo. Inside three months he had achieved eighty hours of flying time in Provosts, twenty-four of them solo. His personal tutor at Cranwell was Squadron-Leader Richard Johns who had worked with the Prince while he was learning to fly Bassetts. It was he who supervised Charles' progress from one front-line plane to the next – by the end of the course Charles had learned to fly Phantom Bombers, Vulcans and Nimrod anti-submarine jets. He had flown over the North Sea on reconnaissance from the Strike Command base at Leuchars, won a good report as co-pilot of a supersonic Phantom fighter and in June 1971 had taken part in a mock attack on Doncaster as pilot of a high-level bombing team flying Vulcans.

In July he had almost completed his course but had done no parachuting, unlike the rest of the cadets. Perhaps the Cranwell authorities were reluctant to take risks with what the Station Commandant described publicly and embarrassingly as 'a precious piece of the nation's property'. Charles prevailed on his mother and some of the air chiefs and he was allowed to undergo training preparatory to making a jump. It was not an obligatory part of the course and he could have gained his coveted wings without jumping. However, as he remarked drily: 'I'm stupid enough to like trying things.'

First there was a spell at the Parachute Training School at Abingdon where he was rehearsed in drill and emergency procedure. Then the great day arrived when, from an altitude of 1200 feet, he was to jump into the sea off Poole. Three other cadets were sent with him in the Andover transport, each of whom was to jump in turn. The day was perfect. A command parachute officer jumped first to test the direction and strength of the wind. He was followed by the officer in charge of the Abingdon school. Finally Flight-Sergeant Kidd said: 'Out you go, sir,' and Charles was in the air. He has given his own account of the 'butterflies in my tummy' before he jumped and, more graphically, of what happened once he had jumped:

Following in his father's footsteps. Charles receives his pilot's wings from Air Chief Marshal Sir Denis Spotswood. The Prince's college reports said he would make 'an excellent jet fighter pilot'.

Happy smiles all round: the Royal Family celebrate the silver wedding anniversary of the Queen and Prince Philip.

Out I went . . . the slipstream is terrific. You appear to be flipped on your back and the next thing I knew my feet were above my head caught in the rigging lines, very odd. I thought, 'They didn't tell me anything about this.' Fortunately my feet weren't twisted around the lines and came out very quickly. The Royal Marines were roaring around in little rubber boats underneath and I was out of the water in ten seconds. A hairy experience. . . .

Prince Charles was awarded his RAF wings and passed out on 20 August 1971. The report declared that he 'will make an excellent fighter pilot at supersonic speeds, has a natural aptitude for flying . . . excels at aerobatics in jets and showed an all-round ability.' His father, wearing the uniform of a marshal of the Royal Air Force, was present at the passing-out parade when Charles received his wings from Air Chief Marshal Sir Denis Spotswood while the band played *God Bless the Prince of Wales.*

During this intensive course the Prince shared a two-floored maisonette with three other officer cadets and his own private detective. He had a bedroom and sitting-room on the first floor, sharing a bathroom with Flying Officer Jim Giles from Wolverhampton. The other two cadets and the detective lived on the ground floor. All five men shared the same batman, taking breakfast in their own rooms before starting on their courses at 8 am. Charles, like all other cadets, had an RAF-issue bicycle to enable him to get quickly from place to place in the widespread camp. He also had a new Aston Martin in which he drove to Belvoir Castle as the guest of the Duke and Duchess of Rutland – and around whose daughter, Charlotte, the press wove yet another fantasy of a love match.

Although he had had little free time and had been obliged to opt out of the Cranwell revue he had found plenty of opportunities for indulging his Goonish sense of humour. On 1 April there was a special announcement over the station's tannoy system expressing apologies from a London shoemaker for faults that had been found in a brand of shoes popular with the cadets. The announcement went on to say that any cadets who owned a pair of these shoes were to bring them to the porter's lodge for modification. A large number of April fools had to thank Prince Charles for their embarrassment!

While he was at Cranwell the Prince was criticized in the *Tailor and Cutter* for his 'cult of shabbiness'. Invited to a master tailors' dinner, he appeared in an old hacking jacket over his dress waistcoat and Order of the Garter. He seemed unaware of the gasps of the immaculately clad tailors until after grace when, to roars of applause, he took off the old jacket to show that he, too, was very correctly dressed.

Charles did manage to visit some of the historic sights of neighbouring Lincolnshire, mingling with other tourists at National Trust sites such as Tattershall Castle, climbing the Boston Stump and wandering around the glorious Lincoln Cathedral. His love for the old and beautiful was, at least, maintained during his hectic few months at Cranwell. He left the college after the passing-out parade for a holiday in Balmoral before going on to Dartmouth in September.

7
The Naval Officer
1971-6

After his short course in the RAF, Charles signed on for a three-to-five year stint in the Royal Navy. He was following in the footsteps of a number of his immediate fore-bears; in 1939 his father had joined the Royal Navy at the age of eighteen and had seen active service during World War II; he had given up his naval career, with some regrets, in 1951 so that he could help Princess Elizabeth take on the increasing burden of royal duties during her father's illness. Charles' beloved grandfather, though a relative failure as a cadet at Dartmouth, had seen active service – as a twenty-one-year-old acting lieutenant he had taken part in the Battle of Jutland in 1916. Charles' great-grandfather, King George V, had served as a naval officer between 1882 and 1892. And, a great influence in royal circles, there was the career of Earl Louis Mountbatten, whose career had included a number of high offices – from Supreme Commander of the Allied Forces in South-east Asia to First Sea Lord (1955–9) and Chief of Staff to the Minister for Defence, a post which he had relin-quished in 1965. Prince Philip had explained why a career in the navy would provide a good training for the future monarch: 'Going to sea is not purely a military opera-tion, it is a professional one. Altogether you live in a highly technological atmosphere, probably a good introduction to the kind of thing which controls our whole existence. And aboard ship you learn to live with people, that is the important thing.'

On 14 September 1971 Charles drove to Dartmouth, arriving there in the evening to meet Captain Allan Tait, the captain of the Royal Naval College. He had a meal in the captain's house where his mother and father had first met in 1939. The new sub-lieutenant slept that night in his cabin, A30, a room on the first floor of the college buildings, with windows looking out on to the sweep of the River Dart. This was to be his base for the six-week course.

The following morning he had to be officially welcomed 'on board' by a party consisting of the Commander-in-Chief of the Naval Home Command, the Deputy

With his great-uncle, Lord Mountbatten, who always took a keen interest in Charles' naval career.

Lieutenant of Devon, the Mayor of Dartmouth and Captain Tait. He was taken from his living quarters by a back door, and driven around the college to the front, where he solemnly shook hands with everyone, assuring them that he had had a long drive from Balmoral. The sense of fun was at work again.

There were three other graduate entrants sharing the course with Charles. Together they were put through a course of square-bashing, seamanship, navigation, marine and electrical engineering, administration, management and all the duties of a divisional officer. They also underwent a period at sea aboard the 360-ton minesweeper *Walkerton*. Once again the Prince was facing a challenge, or perhaps a number of challenges. He had to come to terms with his relative backwardness in things technological, as well as the thought that his father had won the award of the King's dirk as the best special entry cadet of 1939, while Uncle Dickie had come top out of eighty cadets.

The college day began at 6 am and lasted until 10.30 pm and the 'pipe down'. Cadets had a little free time, some of which the Prince spent on the river as one of the crew of a Flying Dutchman, or on the squash court. He also managed to squeeze in weekend visits to friends in Cornwall where he mixed swimming with 'swotting at naval manuals, lying on the beach'. Uncle Dickie flew down to the college for the passing-out parade and noted with pleasure: 'My great-nephew was top in navigation and top in seamanship and that is all we care about.' After the passing-out march-past the two of them flew by helicopter to have lunch with the Queen at Buckingham Palace. In the following week the busy Prince visited Wales for a conservation conference and took part in the State Opening of Parliament. This mixture of service life and royal duties was to be the pattern of his career for the next five years or so.

On 5 November 1971, 'a fiendishly chosen date,' he noted, he flew out to Gibraltar to join HMS *Norfolk*, a guided missile destroyer of about 5600 tons which was engaged on a NATO exercise in the Mediterranean. He was to serve on *Norfolk* for eight months while he worked to gain his naval certificate of competence and a watchkeeping certificate. The Spanish government, hostile to the British in Gibraltar, protested that the Prince's 'presence' unnecessarily offended national feeling and stirred up public opinion. While a crowd of Gibraltarians cheered him on his arrival at Gibraltar airport, the still-raw sub-lieutenant was quickly brought down to reality on board ship. His subordinates had been instructed to 'Sir' him as they would any other officer: his fellow officers addressed him as 'Wales'. Like them he had a small cabin about seven feet square with its standard steel washbasin, wardrobe, bunk and desk. Here he had to work at his studies and compile the junior officer's journal.

On 6 November *Norfolk* sailed, with the new recruit serving as apprentice in the machinery control room, junior assistant at the steering wheel and, after a few days, second officer of the watch. He spent his twenty-third birthday in the Mediterranean, keeping watch during a force ten gale off Sardinia. After playing her part in the winter exercises, *Norfolk* sailed back to Portsmouth, which allowed Charles to spend Christmas with the family at Windsor. Then it was back to work at the shore base, HMS *Dryad*, where he undertook courses in communications, bridgework and gunnery, which he found 'very mathematical'. He took another course at HMS *Dolphin*, a shore base in Gosport where, along with other sub-lieutenants, he learned about submarines. Part of this course involved practising emergency escapes from the bottom of the 100-foot training tank. Some authorities had hinted that the Prince might be excused this hazardous part of the course; he was, after all, not likely to serve as a submariner. But he insisted that, if it was part of the normal course, he had to do it. There were in fact three escapes to be made; one from thirty feet, one from sixty feet and one from a hundred feet – all without the use of breathing apparatus. Charles learned the drill of breathing out, of 'whistling on the way up' during the fifteen-second trip to the surface. The naval and civil press photographers had plenty of pictures to use either as recruiting material or as space-fillers in newspapers.

Norfolk was stationed at Portsmouth during this period and, after Charles had finished his courses at *Dryad* and *Dolphin*, he was sent to sea in the Fleet Air Arm frigate *Hermione* for three weeks to take part in a mock attack on a heavily defended Portland. Then he went back to sea in *Norfolk* which sailed for more NATO exercises in the Mediterranean. The ship docked in Toulon late in May 1972 to enable Charles to join his mother for two days during her state visit to France. When they called on the former Prince of Wales and the Duchess of Windsor, it was clear that the Duke was dying of cancer of the throat. Indeed, eight days later, while *Norfolk* was in Malta for the weekend, Charles' visit to Dom Mintoff, the Maltese Prime Minister, was cut short by a summons to return to Windsor for the funeral of the former King. On Saturday 3 June, following the ceremony of Trooping the Colour, Charles took the bereaved Duchess to see the body lying in state in St George's Chapel at Windsor, thirty-five years to the day on which she and the Duke had married. The Duke was buried in the royal mausoleum at Frogmore where a second space was reserved, on the Queen's instructions, so that the Duchess could eventually be buried alongside the man who had given up his throne for her sake.

At the end of June 1972 *Norfolk* sailed back to Portsmouth at the end of the NATO exercises and, since this was the end of her son's tour with the ship, the Queen went on board 'while I still have the chance'. The Prince showed his mother over the ship and she took tea with the other officers in the wardroom. Having gained his certificates in watchkeeping and naval competence, Charles was now sent on courses at the naval signals school *Mercury*, and on bridgekeeping and nuclear defence at *Dryad*.

During this summer Charles and his grandmother flew by helicopter to the wedding of his twenty-seven-year-old cousin, Prince Richard of Gloucester. Queried as to plans for his own wedding, Charles parried, with a grin, that he was still only twenty-four. Within a month of that happy event the royal family was shocked by the tragic death of the elder of the Gloucester boys, the bachelor Prince William, when his light aircraft crashed during an air race. While this sudden death was still fresh in everyone's mind, it was announced that Prince Charles was to go on a refresher course at the RAF College at Cranwell. The arrangements for this had been made many months before the death of Prince William, but the news that the Prince would be flying a Jet Provost Mark 7 and that one of these had crashed only a week before caused some natural anxiety. However, the course went well, and the Prince flew not only the Provost but also the new Hunter jet fighter. Before returning to Portland for a course in the minesweeper *Glasserton* he went on a week's course on helicopter flying at the naval air base at Yeovilton. He little realized then that this was to be the start of a new and absorbing interest.

Charles' career in the Royal Navy had, necessarily, to be punctuated by the calls of royal duties. In October he attended the training sessions of the Prince of Wales Division in Germany and then went on to appear as guest of honour at a reception held by the West Berlin Senate. From Berlin he flew to spend a few days' holiday on the estates of the Wellesley family in Malaga. The Duke of Wellington's son, Arthur Wellesley, was an army friend who hoped that a few days' shooting would be a pleasant relaxation for the busy Prince. However, the matchmakers of the press noted that he had a younger sister, Lady Jane Wellesley, and so began yet another marriage saga in which the names of Charles and Lady Jane were woven together.

Charles was back at home to celebrate his twenty-fourth birthday and to share, with Princess Anne, the pleasant task of hosting a private supper party to celebrate their parents' silver wedding anniversary on 20 November. For Charles, however, there was a speedy return to naval duties. Almost immediately he was off to join his new ship, the frigate *Minerva*, at Portsmouth. It was a small, general-purpose ship in which the seventeen officers had to perform a wide variety of duties. In February 1973 the *Minerva* sailed for a six-month commission in the West Indies. Charles had already been instructed as to the nature of the royal duties which he would have to perform while serving abroad. The ship stopped over at Bermuda where he met the Governor, Sir Richard Sharples, with whom he discussed some of the political problems facing Bermuda as a result of the forthcoming independence of the Bahamas. Only about a week after this meeting the Governor was assassinated in the gardens where he and the Prince had walked. The dangers which face modern heads of state and politicians were brought home vividly to the reflective Charles.

At the end of May, Charles flew home briefly for the announcement of Princess Anne's engagement to Lieutenant Mark Phillips. He had been promoted to the rank of lieutenant and became second gunnery officer in *Minerva*, which involved the care and maintenance of and practice with the 4.5-inch guns and Seacat missiles. He was also called upon to accept his share of general duties – including the band for the independence celebrations. The crew benefited from his presence on their ship – the people of Nassau who could not come into contact with the Prince himself went out of their way to entertain other members of the crew, treating them, as it were, as stand-ins for the Prince who was busily engaged on his official duties.

The *Minerva* sailed south to the Gulf of Venezuela and then north to Portsmouth in New Hampshire. During the long days at sea Charles experienced the truth of his father's dictum that on board ship 'you learn to live with people'. Charles learned a great deal about his fellow officers and the rest of the crew – where they came from, how they had been educated, what their ambitions were; he heard about their homes, wives, girlfriends, children. In turn he had, necessarily, to reveal much of himself since conversation cannot be one-sided for very long. He had to answer questions about life in the Palace, whether he objected to his lack of freedom to live his own life, when and to whom he was going to get married. By the time *Minerva* returned to Chatham in September at the end of a seven-month tour, Charles' informal education had been taken several stages further.

Charles now had four months at home during which time he was constantly involved in performing royal duties. He undertook a regimental inspection of his own Royal Regiment of Wales. With the Queen away in Australia he took on the role of a Counsellor of State, welcoming new ambassadors to the Palace. When his mother returned home he and Princess Anne drove with her to the State Opening of Parliament, Charles wearing his naval uniform for the first time at a state function. He opened police stations, spoke on conservation at conferences in Wales, visited Bristol and the Scilly Isles and attended a harvest thanksgiving on one of his estates in Somerset. He flew to Luxembourg for a conference – and back again the same evening to attend a charity function for the fund-raising Lord's Taverners in London. Princess Anne's forthcoming marriage led the matchmakers to look for signs that Charles was going to take a step along the same road. When he went off for a short holiday at the Wellesley estate in Spain there were 'exclusive interviews' which 'proved' that an engagement to Lady Jane was 'imminent'. Articles beginning with lines such as 'Bronzed and happy they flew home together . . .' misled the reader by ignoring the fact that there were ten other bronzed and happy people in the home-going plane.

Charles showed that he was upset at these stories and their erroneous conclusions.

He apologized to Lady Jane for the embarrassment, which must have been further increased by the publicity which attended the Wellesleys when they stayed at Sandringham as guests over the New Year. Ten thousand people waited at the estate gates to see the royal family and Lady Jane. As Charles said of this sort of unwelcome publicity: 'It's worse for her than it is for me. I have layers of things to protect me.'

On 2 January he flew from Brize Norton to join his new ship, the frigate *Jupiter*, which was stationed in Singapore. From here he sailed to Australia which, he told guests at a cocktail party, he still thought of as a second home. He really was in a sense almost 'at home', because while he was in Brisbane Prince Philip was in Sydney, stopping over on his way to open the Commonwealth Games in New Zealand on 24 January. At dawn on 29 January *Jupiter* docked in Christchurch, a mere six berths away from *Britannia*, and onlookers had the pleasant sight of the young Prince sprinting along the dockside towards the royal yacht – maybe to wake his still sleeping father. On 30 January the Queen, Princess Anne and Mark Phillips flew to Christchurch to join them.

While the other members of the royal family stayed on in New Zealand, Charles and *Jupiter* sailed again to visit Suva, Samoa, Hawaii and Bega. From here the frigate sailed to the USA where there was great publicity for the Prince of Wales' visit to California. He visited the US Ambassador to London – Walter Annenberg – at his home in Palm Springs, went to Hollywood and met an admiral's daughter, Laura Jo Watkins, who was described as 'tanned, twenty and glossy lipped'. She encountered Charles at a party at a local yacht club and got herself into the news because she had had a fifteen-minute conversation with him. Over-enthusiastic friends assured reporters that 'Laura Jo is a lovely young woman and any relationship with a gentleman would certainly end in marriage.' Charles' ideas on his future bride were somewhat more restrained than that: 'When you marry in my position, you are going to marry someone who perhaps is one day going to become Queen. You have got to choose someone carefully, I think, who could fulfil this particular role and it has got to be someone pretty special. The one advantage of marrying a Princess, for example, or somebody from a royal family, is that they do know what happens.' The unfortunate Laura Jo, misled by the publicity, flew to London in June, by which time Prince Charles was back home. She was a guest at a party given by the Annenbergs at the US Embassy, a party which Prince Charles did not attend. She went to the House of Lords on 13 June to hear him make his maiden speech and for a further three days she stayed on in London, the centre of considerable publicity and press comment. However, at the end of that time, still not having met the Prince again, she flew back to the USA – a very embarrassed young lady.

Charles had completed his service in *Jupiter* early in the summer of 1974. His next course was to be taken at the naval air station at Yeovilton, where he had previously taken a week's course in dual-controlled helicopters. Now in the summer of 1974 he was looking forward to becoming a qualified helicopter pilot. Prince Philip had gained his licence when he was thirty-five. If all went well Charles would get his when he was only twenty-five. And all did go well. There was a ground instruction course lasting fifty-three hours, instruction in dual-controlled machines lasting thirty-eight hours and, finally, a period of at least fifteen hours of solo flight. These were the minimum requirements for a helicopter pilot's licence.

Once again Charles had to cram a great deal into a short space of time; his 105-hour course was to last only forty-five days – 'quite a hard flying rate'. Obviously his experience on fixed-wing aircraft was of some value. But he was quickly made to realize that the helicopter was not an aeroplane. It is an unstable machine which has to be kept under tight control while it makes vertical flight, hovers and manoeuvres. Ten days after first handling the controls, he was off on his first solo flight in a Wessex 5 Commando. He made steady progress at each section of the course, learning, for example, the value of the drills practised on the ground when he had to make an emergency landing after parts of his machine fell off and flames belched from the exhaust. He shut off the engine and coolly brought the crippled machine to land. He also learned to land a machine on the aircraft carrier *Hermes*, a tricky business as he already knew from his experience as a flight deck officer on *Jupiter*, where he had handled the signalling bats and helped pilots to land on deck.

His success was marked at the passing-out parade when he was declared the 'top pilot' of the course. His own description of the course was 'very exciting, very rewarding, very stimulating and sometimes bloody terrifying'. In February 1975, in an interview with the news editor of the *Evening Standard*, he was asked which aspect of his naval career he had enjoyed most. 'I adore flying, and I personally can't think of a better combination than naval flying – being at sea and being able to fly. I think that people who fly in the Fleet Air Arm are of a very high standard. . . . These people are taking all kinds of risks. Taking off and landing on carriers, particularly at night, is no joke at all. . . .'

This was the considered verdict of the pilot who had won the Double Diamond trophy for the student who had made the most progress. The enthusiasm which he felt for the Fleet Air Arm was due in part to the great pride he took in completing his course successfully; there was also an element of family pride. In a foreword which he wrote for a history of the Fleet Air Arm, he noted: 'Pride swells in the heart when I recall the part played by my great-grandfather, Prince Louis of Battenberg, in the formation of the Royal Naval Air Squadron in 1914. Without his interest and enthusiasm and his determined support of the aeroplane versus the airship the Naval

Air Service might quite literally have had great difficulty in getting off the ground.' Charles stayed on at Yeovilton to take an advanced flying course, yet another example of his willingness to accept challenges.

Part of his course was spent at the Royal Marines training school at Lympstone in Devon. Helicopter pilots are frequently called on to carry marines into action, so it is fitting that part of their training should take place over the marines' assault and survival course. Charles had undergone a survival course at Gordonstoun and had become used to swinging hand over hand along the rope over the lake at the school. But he found Lympstone quite different. 'You have to swing over chasms on ropes, slide down ropes at death-defying speed and then walk across wires strung between a pole and a tree.' He added that afterwards he was expected to crawl through tunnels half-filled with mud and run across miles of moor. It was little wonder that he recalled being almost too tired to stand at the end of the day. About this time Prince Philip remarked: 'What a great relief it is when you find that you've actually brought up a reasonable and civilized human being.' He might have commented on the development of that shy young boy who had found it difficult to fit in at Hill House and at Cheam, into the confident, competent and popular young man who had faced and overcome a series of challenges. His fellow-pilots on the course at Yeovilton willingly allowed that he had been best; as a passing-out present they gave him a pen stand made from part of a rotor blade. It stands on his desk at home as a memorial to his ability and a reminder of the good times he had at Yeovilton and Lympstone.

In April 1974 Prince Charles decided to make a permanent home at Chevening, a house which had been made available for his use by a private benefactor. This major decision gave rise to a frenzy of speculation concerning the woman who would become 'the lady of the manor'. Early in 1975 Charles flew with the Duke and Duchess of Gloucester to attend the coronation of the twenty-eight-year-old King Birendra of Nepal in the lovely city of Katmandu. On his return he was due to go on a short course at the Royal Naval College, Greenwich. This, however, was postponed and, instead, he was sent to join 845 Naval Air Squadron with whom he served on the aircraft carrier *Hermes*, which was due to sail to the West Indies and America.

To the gossip writers all was plain. Had not Princess Elizabeth been sent on a long trip to South Africa before the announcement of her engagement to Prince Philip? Had not Katharine Worsley, more recently, gone for a long stay in Canada before she returned for the announcement of her engagement to the Duke of Kent? Similarly, Princess Alexandra had gone on a journey around the world as a prelude to her marriage to Angus Ogilvy. The press confidently asserted not only that such journeys and separations are an almost obligatory part of royal romances, but that *Hermes'* scheduled trips to the West Indies and Canada were, in very deed, the harbinger of the announcement of the engagement that they had all foretold for so long and to so many people.

Charles flew to Devonport to join *Hermes* just two hours before she sailed, landing his naval helicopter on the flight deck which was already cluttered with military equipment and vehicles. He knew some of the people on board, pilots who had been at Yeovilton and marines with whom he had tackled the course at Lympstone. With them and the others he sailed first to the mid-Atlantic to take part in NATO exercises before *Hermes* sailed on to the West Indies. Charles' stay in the Bahamas was cut short because in April he had to go to Canada on an official visit. One again the reception was surprisingly warm. The *Toronto Star* noted 'blue-rinsed matrons nearly pushing police escorts into glass-panelled walls, women dissolving shrieking and quivering as the bachelor heir touched their hands and passed by. . . .' The main reason for this visit was to travel to the North-west Territories so that he could experi-ence life there before the snow and ice had started to thaw. Charles went down a 3500-foot goldmine in Yellowknife and, later, drove a snowmobile to an Eskimo sports meeting. He learned how an igloo was built, and joked with reporters from the comfort of his fur-trimmed parka: 'I hope we don't meet a polar bear, he might think I'm in season.' The press corps made up a song in which they complained of having to try to keep up with him as he made his way 'over the ice floes'. The day after this had first been sung, he composed a song using the Welsh melody used for the hymn *Immortal, invisible, God only wise*; Charles' barber-shop quartet of equerry, physician, detective and secretary sang:

> *Impossible, unapproachable, God only knows*
> *The light's always dreadful and he won't damn-well pose,*
> *Most maddening, most curious, he simply can't fail,*
> *It's always the same with the old Prince of Wales.*

> *Insistent, persistent, the press never end,*
> *One day they will drive me right round the bend,*
> *Recording, rephrasing, every word that I say,*
> *It's got to be news at the end of the day.*

> *Disgraceful, most dangerous to share the same plane,*
> *Denies me the chance to scratch and complain,*
> *Oh where may I ask is the Monarchy going,*
> *When Princes and pressmen are on the same Boeing?*

The programme so formal and highly arranged,
But haven't you heard that it's all been changed,
Friday is Sunday and that is quite plain,
So no one, please no one, is allowed to complain.

But the *pièce de résistance* of this trip came at the underwater research station at Resolute Bay. Here a young scientist, Doctor Joe MacInnis, had claimed a record as the first man ever to swim beneath the North Pole. MacInnis took the Prince down to the Arctic seabed through a hole in the ice which froze almost as soon as they had dived under. The ice was six feet thick, the temperature 28.5 degrees Fahrenheit, and the water was thirty feet deep. Charles, dressed in a diving-suit, looked, as he said, 'like an orange walrus'. He stayed beneath the water for about half an hour, taking photographs with the aid of a lamp. MacInnis joined in the fun, putting on a bowler hat over his diving-suit and carrying an open umbrella upside-down against the ice. Charles enjoyed the trick photography which this enabled him to produce. His own contribution to the fun came when he surfaced, and inflated his diving-suit with compressed air so that he looked massively overweight. The royal family saw TV pictures of this and of the equally ridiculous figure presented as Charles allowed the suit to deflate and shrink as he bowed to the cameras.

Charles returned to *Hermes* which sailed to New Brunswick for a month of helicopter training with the Royal Canadian Air Force at their base at Blissville. Charles left this base in May to fly back to London for his installation as Great Master of the Order of the Bath. The Bath ranks second only to the Garter, of which Charles was already a member, among England's orders of knighthood. It has its origins in a ceremony in which George I had actually bathed with his knights as a token of purity. When he went to the rehearsal on the afternoon after his return from Canada Charles still had his naval 'full set' of beard and moustache. The next morning, wearing his Welsh Guards uniform and simply the moustache, he was solemnly installed by his mother in Henry VII's Chapel in Westminster Abbey. With the other Knights Grand Cross, in their mantles of crimson satin lined with white taffeta, he looked an impressive figure as he promised '. . . to honour God, to be steadfast in the Faith, to love the Queen . . . to defend maidens, widows and orphans in their rights.' The next morning he flew back to rejoin *Hermes* in Nova Scotia. Maybe he had been reminded that naval officers must be either clean shaven or have a 'full set', because the moustache had gone and it was a clean-shaven Charles who flew out from London.

He was back again in London in June to ride, for the first time, in the ceremony of Trooping the Colour which took place that year on the hottest summer day ever

Chatting to an excited member of the crowd when Charles returned to Cambridge in August 1975 to collect his Master of Arts degree. He is wearing the robes which he wore during the ceremony.

recorded, a change indeed from the Arctic cold. While back home he helped to make a film about the British Legion and had an interview with Alistair Cooke which was made into a documentary on George III. He also helped to make a film about Canterbury Cathedral and wrote part of the script for a film on his work as a helicopter pilot.

On 9 February 1976 he took command of his own ship, the *Bronington*, a mine-hunter of 360 tons, with a crew of five officers and thirty-four men. He was only twenty-seven, some two years younger than his father had been when he got his first command on *Magpie*. It was fitting that his ship should be named after a Welsh village, and that it should be one of the smallest ships in the Royal Navy – a reminder to the young commander that he was still a novice in spite of his many duties and honours. The *Bronington*'s main task was to locate mines on the seabed and help divers dispose of them. There were seagoing exercises to be undertaken, during which the new commander had to put into practice some, if not all, of the theory he had learned over the years. When he put into Barry for a three-day visit he once again sported a 'full set' and reminded people of what his grandfather looked like when he was a bearded Duke of York. Perhaps the commander's proudest moment was when he brought *Bronington* to the Pool of London and went to the Palace. He had really come home in style. Unfortunately for him his time as a serving officer was already nearing its end. He had originally joined for a stint of three to five years and this time had already elapsed in September 1976. And in Jubilee Year, 1977, he was going to be called upon to play a major role in organizing both the ceremonies and the Jubilee Appeal. So on 15 December 1976 Charles took leave both of his command and of the Royal Navy, and returned to civilian life.

Charles stands on the bridge of the minesweeper HMS *Bronington*. He had taken command of the ship at the early age of twenty-seven.

8
Chevening

In the spring of 1974 speculation concerning Prince Charles' marriage plans took a new, firmer, turn when it was announced that he had decided to accept the gift of a new home, Chevening, about three miles from Sevenoaks in Kent. An anonymous Palace spokesman tried to head off such speculation with: 'Most young men would expect to have their own home by the time they are his age.' Gossip columnists noted that 'by the time they are his age' most young men are also married.

Charles had his quarters at Buckingham Palace and at the other royal homes in Balmoral, Sandringham and Windsor. When he felt the need to have a country home of his own he bought Wood Farm, not far from Sandringham, which he had found a useful retreat during his time at Cranwell. But if he were to have a place of his own which he could use both as a home and a working base, Wood Farm was too isolated. When he was a young child it had been assumed that he would, one day, become the tenant of Marlborough House, down the Mall from Buckingham Palace, but in 1959 the Queen decided that Marlborough House should become the Commonwealth Centre in London. It was then thought that when Charles made a move from the Palace he would go, as his predecessor, the future Edward VIII, had done, to York House, which is part of the large complex of St James's Palace. But when he was old enough to make this decision he announced that he did not want to live there, and York House has since become the base for a variety of royal institutions, and a London home for the Duke and Duchess of Kent. So by the time that he had finished at Cambridge, Charles still had no real base of his own.

In 1959 Parliament had passed the Chevening Estate Act to meet the wishes of the then Earl of Stanhope who had no children of his own and who wanted to see his family's name remembered in some way. After all, the family had served the country ever since the first of them had earned his earldom after being commander-in-chief of the British forces fighting Napoleon in Spain in 1708. The last of the Stanhope line

Charles has always been a great fan of the Goons, and was only too happy to attend a dinner to celebrate the publication of a book of the famous Goon Show scripts. Here he is sharing a joke with Spike Milligan, Peter Sellers and Michael Bentine. Unfortunately Harry Secombe, the fourth Goon, was ill and could not attend, but he sent the Prince a humorous poem to make up for his absence.

Charles' magnificent home, Chevening House in Kent.

could look back on a glorious family history, for he was not only the last of the Stanhopes, he was also the thirteenth and last Earl of Chesterfield, a title first created in 1628 for a member of the Stanhope family and which this last Stanhope had inherited in 1952 when the last Earl of Chesterfield died without issue. History will remember the third Earl of Chesterfield (1694–1773) as a friend of Voltaire and the object of Dr Johnson's wrath because he had refused to help the lexicographer when he needed assistance to get his great dictionary off the ground.

In 1943 the Earl of Stanhope, who had himself been an active politician – he was First Lord of the Admiralty until 1939, when he became Lord President of the Council – approached Prime Minister Churchill with a proposal that he should make over Chevening 'as a residence for a Cabinet Minister' as he records in his own notes. Chevening had been built by Inigo Jones on the foundations of a Tudor house. The first Earl had acquired it for £28,000 in 1720 when it was already almost a hundred years old, and seven generations of the family had sought constantly to enlarge and improve on the original. So it was a magnificent gift that was being offered.

But in politics little is simple and in matters of property almost all is complicated by legal tangle. So it was not until 1959 that the last Stanhope saw the passing of the Chevening Estate Act. This legalized the trust deed by which he left to the nation the house, its magnificent libraries and paintings along with 3000 acres, as well as a trust fund which was to be either £250,000 or whatever monies he would leave on his death, whichever was the larger sum. In fact the full sum of money under his will proved to be over a million pounds. There was, then, no shortage of money with which to maintain the house and estate.

In the 1959 Act the house was to be offered first to the Queen Mother, who had once stayed there with George VI. Then, if she refused it, it was to be offered in turn to any lineal descendant of George VI, the Prime Minister, other cabinet ministers, the Canadian High Commissioner in London, the US Ambassador, or the National Trust. Following the passage of the Act the Prime Minister, Harold Macmillan, wrote to the Earl: 'Your long service to the State is crowned with a gift which will allow the rare beauty of Chevening and its wonderful atmosphere of peace and serenity to serve the same high purpose which you and your forbears have always cherished.'

But the magnificent house was a mere shadow of its old self. During the war it had been struck by a German bomb, which tore away part of the tile facing and caused cracks to appear in the brickwork. When Prince Charles first saw Chevening in 1969 timbers shored up the walls, the wind rattled every window in the place, and tiles lay around the yards, while inside, the old-fashioned furniture and decoration merely

Wearing full naval uniform, Charles greets a local dignitary during a tribal gathering in his honour in Ghana. An important member of the royal 'firm', the Prince is often called upon to represent the Queen abroad.

seemed to intensify the gloom. An architect's report seemed to confirm Charles' opinion that the gift was not as great as might appear; part of the brickwork was in a dangerous state, and the roof was sagging because of extra chimneys added during Victoria's reign. It would take at least three years' renovation work before the great house could be used.

It is not altogether surprising that the young Prince decided not to exercise the option of taking possession. 'Prince Charles will definitely not be living there,' said the Queen's secretary in January 1973. The first official occupant was Lord Hailsham, Lord Chancellor in Edward Heath's government. He and his wife occupied four rooms in a reconditioned wing while the renovation of the rest of the house went on. Hailsham's tenancy was brief, for the Heath government fell from office in February 1974 and, under the terms of the Act, a political occupant was only entitled to a tenancy while in office. So the trustees went through the list of those entitled to live in the endowed house. Once again the Queen Mother turned down the offer; once again the trustees approached Prince Charles, now twenty-five and, no doubt, already thinking of what he might do once his naval career came to an end. When he went to see the house for the second time in 1974 Charles was both surprised and delighted with the alterations that had been made. Improvements were evident in the appearance of the lawns, trees, lake and fences; the air of decay had been swept away. When he had last seen the house that, too, had been dilapidated and dirty. Now the tiles which had once covered the brickwork had been ripped away and the clean, freshly-pointed brickwork gave the house a new look. The many Victorian attic windows had been torn out and replaced with five dormers. All the windows had been reglazed and the sashes restored to their original eighteenth-century condition and style.

The large central house is linked by curving colonnades to two smaller and beautiful houses or pavilions. Inside the main house Charles was impressed with the pale oak panelling, now cleaned and restored, and with the hanging staircase which twists to the second floor. As in Buckingham Palace, so in Chevening, there are a number of large rooms which may be used only on rare occasions but which are essential if the royal family is to perform its tasks properly. Chevening contains a drawing-room which runs the length of the house; it has a beautifully decorated, intricate Italian plasterwork ceiling, which in 1969 had been covered by layers of dirty off-white paint. The restorers had done their job well in this room with its marble chimneypiece and chandeliers of Waterford crystal. Other rooms hold mementoes of the Stanhopes – gifts from Frederick 1 of Prussia; a Heppelwhite bed in which William Pitt slept when visiting Lady Hester and his other nieces; and a huge Elizabethan four-poster. They all appealed to the historian Prince with his love of things from the past.

Charles was initiated as an honorary chief of the Blood Tribe when he visited Alberta in 1977.

Suitably attired in western gear, Charles watches the famous Calgary stampede with his brother Andrew.

But Chevening had more than beauty to offer. In 1965 the rapidly aging Lord Stanhope wrote of the 'advantage particularly for the heir to the throne to have a residence near London, even Buckingham Palace is being overlooked from all sides and no longer has much privacy.' As he wandered about Chevening Charles appreciated that in this house he could indeed entertain statesmen and diplomats from the Commonwealth, from EEC and other countries. He could house his secretarial staff in one of the linked pavilions while keeping his domestic staff in the other, so that the central block would indeed be both home and office. When he had first walked over the rambling mansion in 1969 it had seemed a mass of rooms linked by miles of passages. Under the careful hands of the restorers and renovators 115 rooms had become 83. The ground floor contains three magnificent reception rooms with a small staff apartment and kitchen. On the first floor is the long drawing-room, a tapestry room and four bedrooms with bathrooms and dressing-rooms. The second floor consists of six bedrooms, four bathrooms, two dressing-rooms and a kitchen, and it was this floor that interested Charles in 1974; he visualized it as the living quarters that he would need if he were to 'live above the shop' as his mother does at Buckingham Palace.

One of Charles' favourite books is an illustrated one which shows Clarence House as it was when it had been restored and renovated for his parents. He has fond memories of that house where he spent part of his childhood, and he has tried to incorporate some of these memories into the redecoration and alterations at Chevening. The house is now completed and has become a centre where he can entertain his friends who live nearby, from which he can work and in which he can arrange meetings of politicians and statesmen. But the house was intended to be more than a bachelor pad. Indeed, that was the point made by his secretary to the last Earl, who died in 1967 before the renovations had even started. But some of his household watched the refurbishing with pleasure. Speaking for most of them, the secretary to the last Earl noted: 'All we need now is for the Prince to find a wife, settle down and have children.'

9
The Future
of the Monarchy

Baiting the royal family is not, as some modern writers might believe, something new. The novelist Thackeray wrote a biting attack on the first four Georges, summing it all up in a short rhyme:

> *George the First was reckoned vile –*
> *Viler still was George the Second;*
> *And what mortal ever heard*
> *Any good of George the Third?*
> *When to hell the Fourth descended,*
> *Heaven be praised, the Georges ended.*

Attacks on Victoria were many, and spanned much of her reign. In 1887 there was an outcry against the financial burden imposed on the British people by the long-reigning Queen and her many children and relations. While the poet Kipling could not be described as a republican, he did criticize Victoria in a poem, *The Widow of Windsor*:

> *'Ave you 'eard of the Widow at Windsor*
> *With a hairy gold crown on 'er 'ead?*
> *She 'as ships in the foam – she 'as millions at 'ome,*
> *And she pays us poor beggars in red.*
> *Walk wide o' the Widow at Windsor*
> *For 'alf o' creation she owns*
> *We have bought 'er the same with the sword an' the flame*
> *An we've salted it down with our bones.*

Popular attitudes towards the British monarchy were changed in the first instance by the ebullient Edward VII, whose reign was too short for him to have made as great an impact as he might have wished. His son, George v, also attracted a great deal of popular support for the monarchy. In one sense this may seem odd since he was above all a very conservative man, correct in all he did, choosing his friends from the narrow band of the landowning aristocracy and never seeking to court public opinion or favour. But he was obviously sincere and meticulous in carrying out his duties. During World War I he made many visits to the front line and was seen to be willing to enter into the spirit and letter of the demands for sacrifice made by Prime Minister Lloyd George.

While his grandmother had been the first to assume the title of Empress, and while he was proud to sign himself 'GRI' in which the 'I' stood for *Imperator* (Emperor), he was wise enough to see that with the passage of time things had to change either peaceably or violently. So in 1931 he willingly accepted the Statute of Westminster, which defined the nature of the British Empire and Commonwealth and which recognized the independence of the Dominions of Australia, Canada, New Zealand and South Africa as equal states united by a common allegiance to the monarch, who was no longer Emperor but King in each of the separate Dominions.

His public image was that of a family man devoted to his wife and children. While later history, particularly the memoirs of his son, the Duke of Windsor, throw doubt on his claim to have been a good father, the public had that impression, and liked it. They approved of his innovation of the Christmas broadcast to the peoples of the Empire and Commonwealth. In this he assumed the role of a father talking to his people and, as he said in one broadcast, 'to the children'. 'I am speaking', he said, 'to the children above all. Remember, children, the King is speaking to you.' In an age which regarded the new wireless as a wonder of science, the relatively un-sophisticated majority of the British people as well as those of the Empire and Commonwealth invested the King with a special aura. There were no latter-day Kiplings or Thackerays to voice doubts. Even his errant son, the Duke of Windsor, critical of his father as a father, had to admit:

> *My father, with the instinctive genius of a simple man, found the means of squaring the apparent circle within the resources of his own character. By the force of his own authentic example – the King himself in the role of the bearded paterfamilias, his devoted and queenly wife, their four grown sons and a daughter, not to mention the rising generation of grandchildren – he transformed the crown as personified by the Royal Family, into a model of the traditional family virtues. . . . The King, as the dutiful father, became the living symbol not only of the nation, but also of the Empire, the last link holding together these diversified and scattered communities.*

Prince Charles wearing the uniform of a Colonel of the Welsh Guards in the Grand Hall of Windsor Castle.

The British people gave George VI a different kind of affection. Widespread sympathy and admiration were shown for the way in which he tackled the job for which he had been unprepared but which was thrust upon him when Edward VIII abdicated. There was vociferous support, though on a small scale, for Edward, who preferred to give up his throne than face the future without being able to marry the twice-divorced Mrs Simpson. The press barons – Beaverbrook and Rothermere – lent their powerful aid to Churchill and others of Edward VIII's circle. But, not for the last time, the press barons had got it wrong. The British people preferred the way in which the new King tackled his unwanted duties to the way in which Edward had preferred self to duty. During World War II George VI and his Queen continued to live 'above the shop', shared in the dangers of the London blitz and went on foot to see the bomb-damaged streets of London, Coventry and other blitzed cities and towns.

During our present Queen's reign there has been a continuation of that monarchi-cal instinct for accepting change and, when it seems desirable, breaking with tradition. She has made many day-to-day changes in the behaviour and practices of the royal family. She gives luncheons at Buckingham Palace to which are invited small, mixed groups of industrialists, politicians, diplomats, trade union leaders, TV stars, journal-ists and other representatives of all walks of British life. In 1957 she abolished the debutante system by which she used to have to sit for hours while hundreds of young girls from 'establishment' families walked slowly past. In the same year she approved of Harold Macmillan's reform of the House of Lords by the creation of life peers and, very innovative, peeresses. She has appeared in more than one TV film. Richard Cawston's *Royal Family* received world-wide acclaim and gave the British people a chance to see the Queen and her family at home. Huw Wheldon's series *Royal Heritage* was not merely a well presented walk through the royal galleries and homes; it was a series which was enlivened by the Queen and other members of the royal family appearing informally to discuss with Wheldon some of their many valuable possessions – paintings, buildings, jewellery and so on.

The Queen has gone out to her people in a way that would have seemed un-thinkable to the 'Widow of Windsor' or indeed to the much less isolated George V. Her walkabouts have become an accepted feature of a royal visit. At the same time she has been jealous of her own privacy, resenting attempts by press or other photog-raphers to break into the activities of the family when they are off-duty. She has also been careful not to become too 'popular', which would create a risk of her losing that 'emotional . . . and mystical' role which the people wish her to play. During her reign Elizabeth II has managed to develop a mixture of aloofness and approachability which was seen at its best during the Jubilee celebrations of 1977. In so doing she has

Charles has always been known for his thoughtfulness and concern for others. This portrait was taken when he led a group of disabled ex-servicemen to the summit of Mount Snowdon.

maintained the monarchical ability to adopt new faces when these are seen to be necessary. For a number of reigns this has been the strong feature of the British royal family, which has neither tried to withstand change nor tried to force the pace.

Speaking in Ottawa in 1952 Sir Winston Churchill declared: 'No political rules can be laid down about the crown. But on the whole it is wise in human affairs and in the government of men, to separate pomp from power.' The political role of the constitutional monarch was defined by Bagehot in his *English Constitution*, in which he claimed that the monarch had the right to be consulted, to encourage and to warn. In order that the monarch may be consulted, he or she receives 'red boxes' every day at home or abroad, whose contents include papers prepared for cabinet committees, memoranda from various ministries and departments, letters and telegrams to and from British diplomats overseas. Elizabeth II is an assiduous and intelligent reader of what must be, by and large, uninteresting material. She makes her own notes, sends for further information whenever she feels she requires it, and is therefore a well-informed monarch. Harold Wilson, who prided himself on his memory, recalled, in his memoirs, that at one weekly audience in 1964 the Queen said, 'Very interesting, this idea of a new town in the Bletchley area.' The Prime Minister had no idea what she was talking about, for he had not read his cabinet papers as carefully as she had – one of them contained the proposal to which she referred. In his retirement speech he said: 'I shall certainly advise my successor to do his homework before audience, and to read all his telegrams and Cabinet Committee papers in time and not leave them to the weekend, or he will feel like an unprepared schoolboy.'

The Queen has also used her position to 'warn' her prime ministers and ministers should the need arise. At first sight it may seem wrong for a constitutional monarch to be involved in such a role. A little reflection enables us to realize that a monarch, particularly one who has reigned for a number of years, may be very well equipped to carry out the task of warning a new prime minister or a thrusting departmental minister. A number of her former prime ministers have written their memoirs. All of them comment on her intelligence, her capacity to ask the right questions, and her grasp of affairs. Churchill used to remark after his weekly audiences, 'What a very attractive and intelligent young woman.' There can be little doubt that when Prince Charles finally comes to the throne he will show the same capacity for hard work as his mother, and that he will bring to his political tasks the intelligence which will be the better developed for the education he has received under her guidance.

The third facet of the monarch's political role is to 'encourage' her ministers, as the Queen's father had encouraged and supported Churchill during the war. Again, the memoirs of her former prime ministers show that she was very ready to fill this supportive role. She alone of a minister's political associates has no interest in helping or hindering anyone's career. She is disinterested and can therefore be trusted as no other political colleague. She let her ministers know that she sympathized with their increasing workload, was concerned when one crisis or another put a strain on a minister and went out of her way to help as far as she could to solve a crisis. A fine example of this was when she helped Harold Wilson during the Rhodesian crisis which blew up in 1965, and ensured by her actions that Ian Smith had no claim to call himself a loyal subject whose only quarrel was with the government.

There is a good deal to be said for assiduous, non-glamorous monarchs who know their role and are prepared to work hard at it. One of the major functions of the Queen in the mid-twentieth century is to act as a link uniting the disparate countries of the Commonwealth. On 29 June 1969 *The Sunday Times* published the results of a poll conducted by Opinion Research Centre. People had been asked to say why they thought the monarchy was important. The percentages of those who subscribed to the various reasons offered were:

Helps keep the Commonwealth united	*69 per cent*
Adds colour to people's lives	*66 per cent*
Makes violent revolution less likely	*64 per cent*
Sets standards of morality	*61 per cent*
Prevents political parties becoming too powerful	*58 per cent*
Sets standards of manners and dress	*52 per cent*

Queen Elizabeth has played that role well. She was the first reigning monarch to visit New Zealand and Australia where, on 3 February 1954, she spoke as Queen of Australia: 'I am proud to be at the head of a nation that has achieved so much.' It was not merely fortuitous that during the conference of Commonwealth leaders held at the time of the 1977 Jubilee, President Kaunda of Zambia should have made a point of praising the way in which the Queen had helped guide the new nations of her Commonwealth through the sticky patch between colonial dependence and self-governing independence. There is little doubt that in the future the monarch will play a different role in the ever-evolving Commonwealth. There were those, in Britain and Australia, who argued that she would not be welcome in Australia which she intended to visit in 1974 and would visit again in 1977. However, the critics were confounded by the warmth of the reception by the Australians who seemed to share the Queen's own view expressed at the Commonwealth Games of 1974 which she opened in New Zealand: 'This is certainly a family gathering. We are glad to be here, and glad to be together. I am sure the same applies to the great family of the Commonwealth.'

On Prince Charles' eighteenth birthday in 1966, an article in the Cardiff newspaper, *The Western Mail*, demanded that 'the prince . . . be given a definite job to do'. The Queen, Prince Philip and the future monarch, together with the 'big five' who met at the Palace in December 1965, rejected such advice. The Prince was allowed to continue with his formal education and then undergo a period in the services. There can be little doubt that when the time comes for him to ascend the throne he will be the best prepared monarch the country has ever had.

The Queen who has given so much thought to his education will wish to avoid exposing her son to the sort of treatment that was meted out to the last two Princes of Wales. Queen Victoria denied her son the chance to undertake any worthwhile duties, although by his own persistence he forced himself on to a commission which examined the problems of working-class housing in 1888. The last Prince of Wales was allowed more opportunity and became, in time, a major figure in Commonwealth countries which he visited frequently and where he was well received. However, he was over-exposed and glamorized, which may well have been a cause of his downfall. The Queen may well choose to give Prince Charles a semi-viceregal role in, perhaps, Australia, New Zealand and Canada. If other leaders of the independent republics inside the Commonwealth share President Kaunda's respect for the monarchy, it may be that the future monarch might, as Prince of Wales, play a role in the affairs of some of these nations. Given the demand from these countries, there seems little doubt that the Prince of Wales would find himself at home as, say, acting head of the Commonwealth. His thoughtfulness, sympathy and interest in people would find an outlet in a role which would enable him to 'be consulted, to encourage and to warn' in these emerging countries.

It was King George VI who said: 'We're not a family, we're a firm.' He was referring to the way in which various members of the family are sent out in an official capacity in answer to the requests and invitations which pour into the Palace. For Prince Philip this has meant hedge-hopping by helicopter from one part of Britain to another, jet-flying to all parts of the world, sometimes alone, sometimes with the Queen. The Queen Mother has been another tireless worker on behalf of 'the firm', but now that she is in her seventies she cannot reasonably be expected to work as hard as the younger members of the royal family – the Gloucesters, the Kents and so on. The Prince of Wales is now the senior of the junior members of 'the firm' and, as such, will take some of this load off his mother and father. Inevitably he will gather his own circle of friends and advisers who will form what will be in effect a junior court. The future Edward VII enjoyed the company of sporting men – and women. The future Edward VIII chose to enjoy a night club life and, as one commentator noted in 1936: 'Unfortunately, among the young people of England, Edward does not know the idealists.' Our future monarch has shown himself to be a thoughtful young man with a sincere concern for the things of the mind, intellect and spirit. There seems little doubt that the composition of his junior court will reflect these deeper interests.

During the years that will elapse before he ascends the throne the Prince will, no doubt, have to read and listen to much criticism of the institution of monarchy as such and the cost of the British monarchy in particular. There seems little doubt that there will be further criticism of his private wealth, built up through the privileged, tax-free provisions made for the monarch and the heir to the throne. It may well be that Charles will have to forgo this privileged position as his predecessors had to give up other of their once-traditional privileges. This will remove one irritant and will be a small price to pay for the maintenance of that respectful affection in which the family and its head are now held.

Prince Charles' future was the subject of that important meeting held at Buckingham Palace in December 1965, during which the Queen discussed her wish to avoid what she called 'an Edward VII situation', and indicated the possibility of her abdicating if and when she felt that Charles could do better. It may well be that the Queen will not wish to keep Prince Charles as an heir-in-waiting, as Queen Victoria kept the future Edward VII. However, there is little evidence that she will, in fact, abdicate. In the broadcast from South Africa on her twenty-first birthday she spoke of dedi-cating 'my whole life, whether it be long or short . . . to your service. . . .' In 1977, during a major Jubilee speech, she referred to that promise and reaffirmed her inten-tion of holding to it. From her father and mother she acquired at an early age a sense of duty, which also served to sustain the two of them in 1936 when, unexpectedly, they were called on to take the place of Edward VIII. From her grandmother, Queen Mary, she acquired from childhood ideas on majesty and duty. When Prince Charles was still an infant, Queen Wilhelmina of Holland abdicated to make way for her daughter, the present Queen Juliana. There seems little doubt that our Queen either heard, or heard of, Queen Mary's critical comment when she was told of the abdication of the sixty-eight-year-old Wilhelmina: '. . . no age to give up your job.'

So there may well be innate pressures for the Queen to carry on. She may also recall her own accession on the sudden death of her father at the relatively early age of fifty-nine. She must have hoped that she would have the opportunity to spend a number of years as the wife of a serving officer in the Royal Navy and as the active mother of a growing family. Instead, after only five years of marriage, and with her elder child less than four years of age, she was brought to the throne and her private life was invaded by the cares of public duty. She may well wish to allow her son and heir the chance to enjoy a longer period of throne-free marriage than she had, and an opportunity to see his own children grow beyond the nursery stage. Whatever her decision in this matter there can be little doubt that Charles will come to the throne intending to honour the motto which now flies on his standard: '*Ich Dien*' – I serve.

Index